Common Phrase Translation:
Spanish for English Speakers

For Occupational Therapy, Physical Therapy, and Speech Therapy

by Jacqueline Thrash, OTR

forewords:

César J. Vallejo, MA, Profesor de español
Guy McCormack, PhD, OTR, Professor
Roger Williams, MPH, RPT, Professor
Ted Levatter, MS, SLP, Professor

Common Phrases Used in Evaluation and Treatment in a Variety of Settings

COMMON PHRASE TRANSLATION:
Spanish for English Speakers

For Occupational Therapy,
Physical Therapy,
and Speech Therapy

by Jacqueline Thrash, OTR © 2006

Publisher:

Jacqueline Thrash
1317 N. San Fernando Blvd # 198
Burbank CA 91504
818-731-5274 cell

thrash@pinkiemae.com
www.livingskillstherapy.com

ISBN 0-9787795-0-9

COMMON PHRASE TRANSLATION:
Spanish for English Speakers

For Occupational Therapy, Physical Therapy, and Speech Therapy

by Jacqueline Thrash, OTR © 2006

forewords:

César J. Vallejo, MA, Profesor de español

Guy McCormack, PhD, OTR/L, FAOTA, Professor

Roger Williams, MPH, RPT, Professor

Ted Levatter, MS SLP, Professor

Sponsored by Glendale Hills Adult Day Heath Care Center
Glendale, CA

Other books available by Jacqueline Thrash, OTR:

Adult Day Treatment Occupational Therapy and Activities Program Manual © 2006

Common Phrase Translation: Spanish for English Speakers For OT, PT, and ST © 2006

OT Categories:

> Categories include: Openings and Closings,
> Evaluation & Treatment: Anatomy, Neuromuscular,
> Activities of Daily Living, Home and Community,
> Self Feeding and Swallowing, Mobility, Orientation,
> Perception, Activities, Precautions: Hip, Weight Bearing UE & LE;
> Swallow; and Encouragement.

PT Categories:

> Openings and Closings, Evaluation & Treatment:
> Anatomy, Neuromuscular, Sensation, Prosthetics, Mobility,
> Wheelchair Mobility, Ambulation, Home and Community,
> Gross Motor Skills, Seated Exercises, Precautions: Hip,
> Weight Bearing UE & LE; Swallow (limited); and Encouragement.

ST Categories:

> Categories include: Openings and Closings,,
> Swallow Evaluation & Treatment, Orientation,
> Perception, Swallow Precautions, and Encouragement.

Coming soon in 2006 & 2007:

Common Phrase Translation: Japanese for English Speakers For OT, PT, and ST
Common Phrase Translation: Korean for English Speakers For OT, PT, and ST
Common Phrase Translation: Mandarin for English Speakers For OT, PT, and ST
Common Phrase Translation: Arabic for English Speakers For OT, PT, and ST
Common Phrase Translation: Armenian for English Speakers For OT, PT, and ST
Common Phrase Translation: Blackfeet for English Speakers For OT, PT, and ST
Common Phrase Translation: Brazilian Portuguese for English Speakers
    For OT, PT, and ST
Common Phrase Translation: Bulgarian for English Speakers For OT, PT, and ST
Common Phrase Translation: Cherokee (Tsalagi) for English Speakers
    For OT, PT, and ST
Common Phrase Translation: Farsi for English Speakers For OT, PT, and ST
Common Phrase Translation: French for English Speakers For OT, PT, and ST
Common Phrase Translation: German for English Speakers For OT, PT, and ST
Common Phrase Translation: Igbo for English Speakers For OT, PT, and ST

Common Phrase Translation: Navajo (Diné) for English Speakers For OT, PT, and ST
Common Phrase Translation: Russian for English Speakers For OT, PT, and ST
Common Phrase Translation: Portuguese for English Speakers For OT, PT, and ST
Common Phrase Translation: Turkish for English Speakers For OT, PT, and ST
Common Phrase Translation: Wolof for English Speakers For OT, PT, and ST

Coming in 2008:

Additional individual languages and

Common Phrase Translation: Occupational Therapy and
Common Phrase Translation Workbook: Occupational Therapy
     (full forty language version)

Common Phrase Translation: Physical Therapy and
Common Phrase Translation Workbook: Physical Therapy
     (full forty language version)

Common Phrase Translation: Speech Therapy and
Common Phrase Translation Workbook: Speech Therapy
     (full forty language version)

For book orders and in-services please contact publisher:

Jacqueline Thrash
1317 N. San Fernando Blvd # 198
Burbank CA 91504

818-494-1148 VM pager

thrash@pinkiemae.com

ISBN 0-9787795-0-9

Front cover design: Pinkie Mae & Co. http://www.pinkiemae.com

What people are saying……

"The thing I like about Jackie is that she tries to understand".
Eddie Thrash, Pinkie Mae & Co, Independent Music Producer.

"Language is for communication and as far as it is open and clear, the process of healing the patient is accelerated and completed. Jacqueline Thrash's enormous effort to build up a bridge of communication through language is not only a wonderful tool, but also already a medicine for the healing of many Hispanic patients who will be grateful to a nurse, a doctor, or a therapist who is able to understand and tries to use their language."
César Vallejo, MA Spanish Literature: Golden Age, Profesor de español, Pasadena City College, CA.

"Jackie Thrash has taken on an enormous task with this manual. I believe that practitioners who will use it with culturally diverse populations will find it enormously helpful because language can be a barrier or a bridge. I highly recommend this manual for your clinical library".
Guy McCormack, OTR/L PhD, FAOTA, Department Chair of University of Missouri-Columbia OT Program, guest editor, and contributor of The Occupational Therapy Manager (2003), author of Pain Management: A Mindbody Approach (1993), and The Therapeutic Use of Touch for Health Professionals (1991).

"A valuable resource for health professionals who are working with multicultural populations. This resource will help bridge the language barrier prevalent in diverse populations as well as develop an appreciation of diverse cultures and their languages".
Roger W. Williams, MPH, PT, Director of Clinical Education, Physical Therapy Program, University of Puget Sound.

"The ability to use a well chosen phrase in a patient's native language should at the very least be a welcome addition to the tool bag of any therapist working in today's nursing home setting."
Ted Levatter, MA CCC SLP, Professor, Speech Department, Glendale Community College, CA.

"What a great idea! Jackie Thrash has created a valuable tool for health professionals who need to communicate with a patient who speaks another language. By creating one book for each profession (OT, PT, ST), Thrash has handily solved a common dilemma through her easy to use multi-translations of common phrases guidebook. Common Phrase Translation should be a 'must have' for every acute or rehab therapist".
Norine Dresser, Adjunct faculty CSU Los Angeles, folklorist/author of Multicultural Manners.

"Communication is essential to competent health care and health care research. Jacqueline Thrash's <u>Common Phrase Translation</u> (OT/PT/ST) is a welcome tool for building rapport when providing health services as well as conducting health research among populations where language is a barrier. Medical and biological anthropologists as well as social workers, psychologists, nurses and physicians working in hospitals and clinics with linguistically-mixed populations will find this work particularly helpful."

> Kevin M. Kelly, PhD, Associate Research Scientist, College of Public Health, Adjunct Associate Professor, Dept of Anthropology, Department of Community & Behavioral Health, and Department of Occupational & Environmental Health at the University of Iowa. Webmaster of http://www.Plagiocephaly.org

"As a prior student of mine, Jacqueline has demonstrated an exceptional scholastic ability and passion for research regarding the nexuses of language, culture and therapy. Her book, <u>Common Phrase Translation</u> is an example of this passion, and will be valuable to researchers, educators, and clinicians".

> Michael J. Carter, PhD, Professor, Anthropologist; Glendale Community College, and LA Valley College.

"Creating rapport is essential to providing culturally competent health care. When the patient does not speak fluent English, this can be a very challenging task. Jackie Thrash has written an extremely helpful book in that regard. It will enable occupational therapists and others to communicate their interest in their patient by showing that they've taken the time to learn a few of the social niceties in their language. Thrash has done an incredible job of compiling important words and phrases in numerous languages".

> Geri-ann Galanti PhD, Associate Professor, CSU Los Angeles, Department of Anthropology, and CSU Dominguez Hills, Department of Nursing, and author of <u>Caring for Patients from Different Cultures</u>.

"Jacqueline Thrash's <u>Common Phrase Translation</u> is a much needed and appreciated tool for use in rehab therapy. It provides the therapist with increased communication skills in working with clients of multi-linguistic and cultural backgrounds and is a more effective treatment in that it enables the client to feel more comfortable using his native language in a potentially foreign/alien or isolated environment".

> Elaine Sinclair, SLP/Rehab Coordinator, Sinclair and Associates.

"In Europe, we are likely to meet many foreign people (residents, tourists, and therapists). This workbook can be useful to understand and be understood by them. It allows the international therapist (and students) a larger variety of languages needed to work with many different people. It also allows for travel and work in other countries. This gives us more possibilities, opportunities, and experiences. It is my pleasure to be involved in this international project".

> Nadia Crivelli, OT Student, native Italian speaker. (Parabiago Italy).

"Jackie Thrash's <u>Common Phrase Translation</u> fills a significant gap by offering translations specific to the needs of occupational, physical, and speech therapy in an impressive variety of languages. Her thorough and meticulous work reflects her own knowledge of and background in rehabilitation as well as an abiding concern for the importance of communication in ensuring the success of physical rehabilitation for all patients, regardless of ethnic or linguistic background. I look forward to the expansion of this project as she continues to add more and more languages to this most important resource."
    Derek B. Milne, Instructor, Anthropology, Pasadena City College, CA.

"Jackie's <u>Common Phrase Translation</u> for OT, PT and ST is not a book elaborating on how to learn a foreign language, but rather a communication tool for those in the therapy field. To hear the therapist or nurse speaking the same language will draw close between the patient and the therapist or nurse, even if the same language has some "foreign" accent. I highly recommend this manual."
    Paul Ge, MBA, Former Chinese Language Instructor.

"Through her work with persons from immigrant populations, Jacqueline Thrash realized an urgent need to help therapists gain competence in serving persons whose primary languages differ from English. Jacqueline channeled her passion for helping people and her strong interest in anthropology, linguistics and culture, and initiated the development of this comprehensive multi-lingual resource directory for Occupational, Physical, and Speech Therapists. This directory will no doubt prove indispensable to therapists, and serve as a vehicle to improve the delivery of services to a multitude of patients".
    Mark Sakata, MS, CRC, Teacher Specialist-Disabilities,
    Pasadena City College, CA.

"Language is a powerful tool and can improve the relationship between patient and professional, the sick and healthy."
    Judith Fogle, MA, Professor of Germanistik, head of German Studies
    Program, Pasadena City College.

"Much more accurate and effective communication, assessment, and client care should be possible through the use of <u>Common Phrase Translation: Spanish for English Speakers</u>. This book can greatly facilitate the achievement of cultural competence and is, therefore, an excellent resource for all health professionals".
    Lela A. Llorens, PhD., OTR, FAOTA
    Professor Emerita, Department of Occupational Therapy, San Jose State
    University; Core Faculty Emerita, Stanford Geriatric Education Center,
    Stanford University; Adjunct Professor, Division of Occupational Science
    and Occupational Therapy in the School of Dentistry, University of
    Southern California.

Dedicated in memory of my parents,
Allan D. Bell Jr, and Clare E. Summers,
and to those native Spanish speakers
who have shared their culture and language
with me over the last 30 years,
especially Mark Gomez, and Rachel Cano.

<u>Acknowledgements</u>

First of all, I must acknowledge that all glory goes to my creator, for without him nothing I do is possible.

Also, I am especially thankful, for <u>over</u> a year ago, I was struck by a van and sustained multiple fractures, and lived to tell about it. This gave me yet another opportunity to practice occupational therapy (on myself). I have used the writing of this book as therapy both for my physical disabilities as well as the associated mental effects.

Praise goes to Dr. Neil Ford Jones, of UCLA, chief hand surgeon, and Dr. Neil Harness, assisting hand surgeon, for perfect reconstruction of my right wrist bones, and ligaments. Thanks to my PTs at Synergy and St. Joseph's, and especially to my hand therapists, Tina and Alice.

Second, I would like to thank (post humus) my parents, Allan D. Bell Jr., and Clare E. Summers for their encouragement of the gifts and curiosities put into me by my creator. My mother, was also valedictorian of her high school despite a year long bed bound illness, in 1945.

Third, I would like to extend *special thanks* to my husband, Eddie Thrash, who accepts my human imperfections while encouraging me to be the best I can be. Also, he taught me how to produce a work and copyright. http://www.pinkiemae.com

Fourth, I would like to thank the following educators and authors for their encouragement, cultural education, and guidance with this project.

Guy McCormack, OTR PhD, FAOTA, Department Chair of OT Program, University of
      Missouri-Columbia, author of <u>Pain Management: A Mindbody Approach</u> (1993),
      and <u>The Therapeutic Use of Touch for Health Professionals</u> (1991).
Roger Williams, MPH, RPT, Director of Clinical Education, Physical Therapy Program,
      University of Puget Sound.
Ted Levatter, MA CCC, SLP, Professor of Speech, Glendale Community College, CA.
Ray Richardson, Ph D, Laney College African American Studies Department Chair
Geri-Ann Galanti, PhD Anthropology Associate Professor, CSU Los Angeles,
      Department of Anthropology and CSU Dominguez Hills, Department of Nursing
      and author of <u>Caring for Patients from Different Cultures</u>.
      http://www.calstatela.edu/faculty/ggalant/
Norine Dresser, CSU Los Angeles, Adjunct Faculty, MA Folklore/Mythology, author of
      <u>Multicultural Manners</u> and <u>Multicultural Celebrations</u>.
      http://www.norinedresser.com
Kevin M. Kelly, PhD, Associate Research Scientist, College of Public Health, Adjunct
      Associate Professor, Dept of Anthropology, Department of Community &
      Behavioral Health, and Department of Occupational & Environmental Health at
      the University of Iowa. http://www.Plagiocephaly.org
Michael J. Carter, PhD, Cultural Anthropologist, Glendale Community College, CA.

Common Phrase Translation: Spanish for English Speakers For OT, PT, & ST ii

Wendy Fonarow, PhD, Anthropologist, Glendale Community College, CA author of
    Empire of Dirt: The Aesthetics and Rituals of British Indie Music (2006)
    http://www.glendale.edu/anthropology/fonarow.htm
Derek Milne, MS, Anthropology Instructor, Pasadena Community College, CA.
Lauren Arenson, PhD Professor Anthropology, Pasadena Community College, CA.
Mikel Hogan, PhD, Anthropology Professor, California State University-Fullerton, CA.
Elizabeth Cara, OTR, PhD, Associate Professor, San Jose State University Occupational
    Therapy Program, http://www2.sjsu.edu/ot/ edcara@casa.sjsu.edu
George Tomlin, OTR PhD, Department Chair of University of Puget Sound OT Program
Juli McGruder, OTR PhD, Professor of University of Puget Sound OT Program
Laura Mastumoto, MS, OTR/L, High tech specialist and instructor, Glendale Community
    College, CA.
Mark Sakata, Teacher Specialist, Academic Advisor, Pasadena City College, CA.
Susan Hunkins, PhD Education.
Gheith Effarah, RPT, MBA, Director of Operations interface rehab inc., Consultant.
Larry Wren, RPT, and Carol Wren, RN.
Janice Wexler, VITA, Los Angeles, CA.
Wendell Cooper, Department of Rehabilitation, Burbank CA.
Sang Park, Prowalk Orthopedics, Van Nuys, CA.
Staff at High Tech Centers, GCC, and PCC, CA.
Staff at UCLA Department of Orthopedics, Westwood, CA.

Lela Llorens, OTR PhD, FAOTA, Retired Professor and author, Developing Ego
    Functions in Disturbed Children: Occupational Therapy in Milieu.
Gordon Burton, OTR, PhD, FAOTA, Retired Professor and author.

César J.Vallejo, MA Spanish Literature: Golden Age, Profesor de español,
    Pasadena City College, CA.
Paul Ge, MBA, Former Chinese Language Instructor.
Judith Fogle, MA, Professor of Germanistik, Pasadena City College, CA.

Yale University Press for research material: An Introduction to Spanish for Health Care
    Workers.
Baja Books for research material: Speedy Spanish for Physical Therapists, and Speedy
    Spanish for Medical Personnel, and Speedy Spanish for Public Health Personnel.
Slack Inc. for research material: The PTA Handbook: Keys to Success in School and
    Career for the Physical Therapy Assistant.

Fifth, I would like to thank all of the hundreds of people who, over my lifetime (nearly 50
years) have shared their culture and languages with me. I would like to mention a few
specifically:

Eddie & Jennifer Thrash, (African American), Eddy Emilien and MC, (French
Guadaloupe & France), Karmen Keshishian, (Armenia), Christian Achikam, OTR,
(Nigeria) Reshmi Saraladevi, SLP (India), Lucy Escobar, PTA (Mexican American),

Jacqueline Thrash, OTR

Yoshiko "Hiyoko" Ezawa, (Japan), Lucy, RPT (Uganda), Mark Gomez and family (Mexican American), Rachel Cano, LVN, (Mexican American), Naomi and Zak Diouf, West African Dancers and Choreographers (Senegal). Marilyn Bates & Marvin Williams (Navajo).

The staff at Glendale Adult Day Treatment Center, in Glendale CA (Armenia, Iran, Russia)

The housekeeping and general staff at Ramada Inn Burbank (Mexico, El Salvador, & Mexican American)

Special Thanks goes to Maya Hingorany, MS CCC SLP, and Reshmi Saraladevi, MS CCC SLP, for assistance with the Speech Therapy Phrases; and Lucy Escobar, PTA for assistance with the Physical Therapy Phrases.

Last but not least, I would like to thank the numerous translators (credited at each chapter) who worked tirelessly and generously on this project. I could not have done it with out you (all).

This project has been a joyful and therapeutic labor of love.

Jackie.

Jacqueline Thrash, OTR

Table of Contents

Acknowledgements i
Table of Contents v
Forewords ix
Preface xiii
How to Use this Book xv

Spanish for English Speakers: Occupational Therapy 1
   Openings and Closings 3
   Evaluation 5
      Anatomy 8
      Neuromuscular 9
      Activities of Daily Living 10
      Home and Community 10
   Treatment 11
      Activity of Daily Living 11
      Self Feeding and Difficulty with Swallowing (Dysphagia) 11
      Neuromuscular 12
      Mobility 13
      Orientation 13
      Perception 14
      Activities 15
   Precautions 16
      Hip Precautions 16
      Weight Bearing: Upper Extremity 16
      Weight Bearing: Lower Extremity 16
      Swallow Precautions 17
   Encouragement 17
   Notes 19

Spanish for English Speakers: Physical Therapy 21
   Openings and Closings 23
   Evaluation 25
      Anatomy 28
      Neuromuscular 29
      Sensation 30
      Prosthetics 30
      Mobility 31
      Wheelchair Mobility 32
      Ambulation 32
      Home and Community 34
   Treatment 35
      Neuromuscular 35

Prosthetics 36
Mobility 38
Wheelchair Mobility 39
Ambulation 39
Gross Motor Skills 41
Ball Toss 41
Ring Toss 42
Ball Kicking 42
Seated Exercises 42
Upper Extremity 42
Lower Extremity 43
Precautions 44
Hip Precautions 44
Weight Bearing: Upper & Lower Extremity 44
Swallow Precautions 45
Encouragement 46
Notes 47

Spanish for English Speakers: Speech Therapy 49
Openings and Closings 51
Evaluation 53
Swallowing Evaluation and Treatment 55
Orientation 57
Perception 58
Swallowing Precautions 59
Encouragement 59
Notes 61

Theory 63
Background 63
History 64
What is Cultural Competency? 66
Why is Cultural Competency Important? 67
Medical Anthropology & Allied Health (OT/PT/ST) 70
Cultural Interfacing 72
Review of Literature 76
References 79

Broadening Your Horizons 81
Languages and Culture 81
Linguistics and Linguistic Anthropology 81
Languages and Countries 82
References 84

Jacqueline Thrash, OTR

Learning Social Greetings in Multiple Languages 85
    References 89

Conclusion 91

FULL VERSION TRANSLATION LIST 93

Appendices A & B 95
    Appendix A 97
        Africa 97
        The Americas 98
        Asia 100
        Europe 101
        The Pacific 103
    Appendix B 105
        Administration on Aging 105
        Anthropology 105
        Cultural Awareness 105
        Health and Human Services 106
        Language 106
        Medical Care 106
        Nursing 108
        Occupational Therapy 108
        Physical Therapy 108
        Speech Language Pathology 109

About the Authors 111
    Jacqueline (Bell) Thrash 111
    César J. Vallejo 111
    Guy McCormack 111
    Roger W. Williams 112
    Ted Levatter 112

Jacqueline Thrash, OTR

<u>Foreword by César J. Vallejo, MA, Profesor de español.</u>

What a sense of relief a patient could experience if a doctor, nurse, or therapist understands and communicates with him or her in his/her own language! I have witnessed this kind of feeling when some members of my own family haven't been able to communicate in English, and the health professionals knew Spanish. When a physician, nurse, therapist, or caretaker has tried to communicate in Spanish, my relatives have been able to understand directions and commands. Staff use of Spanish communication helped my family express their concerns, fears, and emotions. When the therapists, caregivers, and nurses spoke in Spanish to my 89-year-old father-in-law at a convalescent home, he responds much better to directions and instructions. This helped him recover more rapidly from the stroke that put him in a wheelchair for almost eight years.

Jacqueline Thrash's book, <u>Common Phrase Translation</u>, in so many languages is without a doubt the beginning of the cure for many patients of different cultures. The Spanish speaking community particularly will benefit from their health professionals who will take care of them in all situations of illnesses, whether nurses, speech therapists, physical therapists, or occupational therapists, who communicate in Spanish. On behalf of my community, I thank Jacqueline and the rest of professionals who have contributed to this endeavor. Congratulations.

César J. Vallejo.

<u>Foreword by Guy McCormack, PhD, OTR/L, Professor</u>

One of the most gratifying experiences of being a teacher is to have a former student succeed and stay in touch with you. Jacqueline (Bell) Thrash was a student of mine in 1984-1986 in the Department of Occupational Therapy at San Jose State University in San Jose, California. Jacqueline or Jackie as we addressed her was not a typical student. She had vast life experience, creativity, and an enthusiasm for learning. Her enthusiasm and quest for knowledge continues to this day.

Jackie Thrash has taken on an enormous task with this manual. I believe that practitioners who will use it with culturally diverse populations will find it enormously helpful because language can be a barrier or a bridge. Language becomes a barrier when two people from different cultures and ethnic/racial backgrounds try to communicate without a common dialect. By simply saying a few words, albeit perhaps poorly pronounced words, you can go a long way in bridging the communication gap. Thus, verbal and of course non-verbal communication is an integral part of the therapeutic process.

I became aware of the importance of language on a recent trip to China. I was with a small team of Americans visiting the Third People's Hospital in Chungqing, China. Our mission was to represent the University of Missouri to establish and sustain relationships and staff exchanges between our two hospitals. I was asked to give power point presentations on topics in rehabilitation and to treat patients in the hospital from an Eastern and Western perspective. Although touch is a universal communicant, it became clear the oral communication was necessary to obtain the patient's history, diagnosis, and current complaints about their conditions. Although we used interpreters to translate oral communication, the exchange of information and the meaning of certain things were inconsistent and open to misinterpretation. If I had a copy of Jackie's manual and a few Cantonese expressions, I may have advanced my communications and made the therapeutic interventions more effective.

In conclusion, the information contained within this manual is most useful because we are living in a global community. Practitioners are challenged to be culturally competent today. More and more people of diverse backgrounds are entering the American health care system every day. Contained within this manual is a vast collection of the common phrases used in occupational therapy practice. These phrases have been translated into 35 different languages. I grant some of the terms are difficult to pronounce, but any attempt to use the person's native language conveys respect and an interest in their culture. Even badly pronounced terms often bring comic relief and allow the patient to educate the practitioner and the intervention becomes more client-centered.

I highly recommend these manuals for your clinical library.

Guy McCormack

Jacqueline Thrash, OTR

Foreword by Roger W. Williams, PT, MPH, Professor

I am truly honored to provide a foreword for Jacqueline (Bell) Thrash's text. In her full forty language text of <u>Common Phrase Translation</u>, she has translated different languages in order to meet the diverse cultural and language needs of the patients we all serve. She has also included a series of individual language texts by the same name.

 As director of clinical education for the physical therapy program at the University of Puget Sound, my students have worked in a variety of clinics in many states (WA, AK, OR, CA, HI, ID, MT, MN, NV, CO). Each of the represented facilities in these states has seen patients who come from a variety of countries, requiring the students to interpret and understand patients who demonstrate multi languages and dialects and represent diverse cultures. Both students and patients have used a variety of communicative means (gestures, pictures, pantomimes) to explain, understand and communicate their treatment needs. This text provides common occupational therapy, physical therapy, and speech therapy phrases, translated into up to 40 languages and bridges the gap created by this language and cultural diversity.

 Attempting to "learn" and "speak" the language of others shows respect for the person and his/her culture. Any opportunity to connect with our patients will bring the people of our diverse culture together for the common good of all.

 I highly recommend these texts for any therapist interacting with people of the world. The common phrases that are included within each text will be starting point to assist in communicating with our non-English speaking patients.

 Thanks for asking me.

 Roger Williams

Foreword by Ted Levatter, MA CCC, SLP, Professor

Having spent several years working as a speech therapist in the nursing home setting. I can say without reservation that it is one of the most demanding and stressful situations in which one can work. In addition to working with patients with often life and death medical issues in a frequently less than ideal environment, therapists must also face the challenge of an increasingly culturally and linguistically diverse patient population. All too often, the challenge of overcoming a language barrier between patient and therapist is the single most important factor in a less than successful outcome. While not solving this problem completely, Jacqueline (Bell) Thrash's manual is an important step in the right direction. The ability to use a well-chosen phrase in a patient's native language should at the very least be a welcome addition to the tool bag of any therapist working in today's nursing home setting.

While clearly valuable in working with patients who have suffered impaired communication skills due to a stroke, this manual should make an even more crucial difference when working with dysphagia patients. Any therapist who has worked in the nursing home setting has been faced with the frustration of not being able to communicate clearly and effectively with a patient faced with a life threatening swallowing deficit in a timely manner without the need for a family member or other interpreter to be present.

While Ms. Thrash's work has the potential to make a difference in the quality of life of many patients, it should also give the therapist new power to communicate essential information and to perform a difficult job with greater autonomy. I highly recommend this manual to any therapist working in the acute care, nursing home, and home health settings in hope that it will prove to be an essential tool in helping to face the challenge of an increasing multilingual patient population in the years to come.

Ted Levatter

Jacqueline Thrash, OTR

Preface

Inventions are born out of necessity. I know this, personally, because both my maternal grandfather, Harry Summers, and my father, Lt. Col Allan Bell Jr. were inventors. I, also, have dabbled in it. My grandfather, while working for Columbia in 1923, invented the electric stylus (needle) on the record player. My father, while working in Counterintelligence for the U.S. Army, and afterwards, invented spy gadgets (voice lie detector, concealed lock picking device, and microdot camera, to name a few) to make his job easier.

This book, <u>Common Phrase Translation: Spanish For English Speakers For Occupational Therapy, Physical Therapy, and Speech Therapy</u>, is extracted from the full forty language versions: *Common Phrase Translation: Occupational Therapy, Common Phrase Translation: Physical Therapy, and Common Phrase Translation: Speech Therapy*. While writing the full forty language versions, I realized that there could be an interest in the one language version. For instance, an individual therapist may want all 40 languages, or s/he may only need one or two. I have put OT, PT, and ST, together in a single language version (Spanish, Armenia, Russian, etc.) so that a clinic or rehab department can share, or a therapist can show his or her colleagues what is available.

Regardless of which version you are reading, all of them were born out of necessity. Their seeds, however, were planted over 40 years ago-when I was a child.

In the early 1960s we lived in Germany: Berlin and Stuttgardt. Both of my brothers learned German in the Army school. Even though I was a toddler and then a small child at the time, I learned to say and respond to: good morning, good night, thank you, you are welcome, sleep good, come here please, and sit down please. Oh yes, and dumb head (my brother, Dirk, called me that). Later, in 1967 and 1968, my father spent two summers in Madrid, Spain and Corfu, Greece teaching the (then) Prince Juan Carlos of Spain and (exiled) King Constantine of Greece Kung Fu. He brought back a few more saying to add to our daily repertoire. The seed was firmly planted.

Over the years, I continued to seek out and add new phrases, from Japanese, Cantonese, Mandarin, Korean, Spanish, French, Italian, Russian, Wolof, and Swahili. Later, as a practicing registered Occupational Therapist, I noticed that my non-English speaking clients appeared uneasy in unfamiliar surroundings. I tried my simple phrases on them (in their language) and Voila! Their faces lit up and they relaxed and appeared to trust me more. I kept doing this with different ethnic groups, and had the same positive results.

The necessity. What if I had a book with common OT (PT/ST) phrases translated into 20 or 30 different languages? If so, I could say more than "Hi, how are you?" in 20 to 30 languages just by cracking open the book. But alas, I couldn't find one; so I wrote it. I had good mentors. In addition to my father and grandfather's inventiveness, my mother was valedictorian of her high school graduating class of 1945; and my husband, Eddie Thrash, of Pinkie Mae & Co. has independently published CDs and a booklet.

This is the prototype of this project. Ultimately, a book like this would cover all available languages (and even each dialect within each language). But, I figured it was best to get it started and out in the world. A project such as this takes years to develop (from seed to blossom). It also takes many, many people's contribution, influence, and encouragement. Please see previous section for acknowledgments.

I realize that, normally, in educational and professional literary works, the personal pronouns "I" and "you" aren't used; the author and reader are usually referred to by those nouns. Because this is a book about culture, people, and communication between peoples, I have chosen to use I when describing my experiences, and you when speaking to the reader.

Please refer to the How To Use This Book section for further guidance.

Jacqueline Thrash, OTR

How to Use This Book

This book, <u>Common Phrase Translation: Spanish For English Speakers For Occupational Therapy, Physical Therapy and Speech Therapy</u> has been divided into eight sections: Front Matter (Acknowledgements, Preface, Forewords, Table of Contents, How to Use This Book); Translations: OT, PT & ST; Conclusion, Theory, Broadening Your Horizons, Learning Social Greetings in Multiple Languages; Appendices, and About the Authors.

Translations: (OT, PT, and ST) is the largest section of the book. This section contains the entire phrase files for occupational, physical, and speech therapy. Combined they include over 900 phrases, however, there is some overlap between the disciplines.

Conclusion

Theory is further broken down into Background, History (including Civil Rights), What is Cultural Competency? Why is Cultural Competency Important?, Cultural and Medical Anthropology, Cultural Interfacing, Review of Literature, and References.

Broadening Your Horizons discusses linguistics and linguistic anthropology, and languages. It lists thirteen common languages, and the countries in which each language is spoken. i.e. **Swahili** Democratic Republic of Congo, Kenya, Rwanda, and Tanzania.

Learning Social Greetings in Multiple Languages lists two social greetings from each of the up to 40 language: How Are You? I'm Fine, Thank You, listed alphabetically, by language.

I have <u>transliterated</u> many of the languages so that they can be "read" by English speaking therapists. These include but are not limited to: Amharic, Arabic, Armenian, Bulgarian, Farsi, Greek, Hindi, Japanese, Korean, Mandarin, Russian, Thai, Turkish, and Vietnamese.

Appendix A is cross-reference of Country and Languages (reverse of Languages & Countries). It is to be used by the therapist in order to find out what languages are spoken in a specific country. It includes the number of living languages, and the specific languages present in this book. i.e. Algeria, 18 living languages spoken in the country, and Arabic and French present in this book. So, if you find out that you have a patient from Senegal, and don't have a clue what languages are spoken in that country, you can look it up.

Appendix B is Cultural Competency Resources. It includes websites and associated seminars which can be used to further your education in this area.

About the Authors tells about Jacqueline (Bell) Thrash, César Vallejo, Guy McCormack, Roger Williams, and Ted Levatter.

How to Use this Book:

1. Scan the table of contents
2. Locate the discipline you are interested in.
3. Find the phrase category (such as evaluation, treatment, neuromuscular, swallowing, activities of daily living, etc.)
4. Flip to that section in the book.
5. Scan the phrases for the few you want.
6. Read them aloud to yourself a few times.
7. You can copy them down on your clipboard for quick reference, or bring the book into the patient's room or the clinic during evaluation and treatment.

For example:

Speech Therapy: Swallow Evaluation—page 55.
"My name is Reshmi. I am a speech therapist. I am going to give you something to eat and drink".

Or:

Occupational Therapy: Activities of Daily Living—page 11.
"My name is Jacqueline. I am an occupational therapist. Would you like to brush your teeth? Can you do it? I will help you".

Or

Physical Therapy: Evaluation—page 27.
My name is Larry. I am a physical therapist. I need to see how you can walk".

Jacqueline Thrash, OTR

Note from author:

I expect that there may be some typographical errors, in English, or in the translated languages. If you find any, please email me (or postal mail) and I will make corrections for the next printing. I have not been able to include all of the languages from all of the countries of the world. If I have missed your language, I apologize. Please email me, or write a postal letter, and maybe we can work your language into the next printing.

thrash@pinkiemae.com

My postal mailing address can be found at all times on the following website

http://www.pinkiemae.com/contact_us.htm

Feel free to write. Jacqueline Thrash OTR/L

Post Script: I know it may be tempting to photocopy this material, however, besides being illegal (all rights reserved), it is also disrespectful to the hard work of the author and translators, as well as the publisher. Please, if you need another copy, or want to share it with your colleagues, email Jacqueline Thrash, and ask for a discount on the second copy.

Jacqueline Thrash, OTR

OCCUPATIONAL THERAPY

OT ENGLISH TO SPANISH (LATIN) by Jacqueline Thrash, OTR © **2006**

OPENINGS AND CLOSINGS:

1. Good Morning	1. Buenos días.
2. Good Afternoon	2 Buenas tardes.
3. Good Evening	3. Buenas noches.
4. Good Night	4. Buenas noches.
5. Thank you.	5. Gracias.
6. What is your name?	6. ¿Cual es su nombre?
7. My name is Jacqueline.	7. Mi nombre es Jacqueline. OR Me llamo Jacqueline.
8. Do You Speak English?	8. ¿Habla usted inglés?
9. Does anyone here speak English?	9. ¿Alguien aquí habla inglés?
10. Excuse my poor Spanish.	10. Disculpe mi español.
11. I only speak a little Spanish.	11. Yo sólo hablo un poco de español.
12. I am sorry, I do not speak Spanish.	12. Lo siento, yo no hablo español.
13. Can you speak more slowly?	13. ¿Puede hablar más despacio?
14. Yes	14. Sí
15. No	15. No
16. Please	16. Por favor
17. Thanks	17. Gracias
18. Mister	18. Señor
19. Missus	19. Señora
20. Miss	20. Señorita

21. You are Welcome	21. De nada.
22. Excuse Me	22. Disculpe.
23. I Am Sorry	23. Lo Siento.
24. This is Clare.	24. Ésta es Clara.
25. How Are You?	25. ¿Cómo está usted?
26. How Have You Been?	26. ¿Cómo ha estado?
27. I am fine. Thank you.	27. Yo estoy bien. Gracias.
28. I am very glad to meet you.	28. Mucho gusto en conocerle.
29. It was nice meeting you.	29. Fue un placer conocerle.
30. What did you say?	30. ¿Qué dijo?
31. Have a nice day.	31. Que tenga un buen día.
32. That's all right.	32. Eso esta bien.
33. I understand you.	33. Yo lo entiendo. (you-male) Yo la entiendo. (you-female)
34. I do not understand	34. Yo no entiendo.
35. I understand perfectly.	35. Yo entiendo perfectamente.
36. I understand you very well.	36. Yo lo entiendo muy bien.
37. Fine, thanks. How is your family?	37. Bien, gracias. ¿Cómo esta su familia?
38. See you later.	38. Hasta luego.
39. See you tomorrow.	39. Hasta mañana.

40. This is my husband (name), my daughter (name) and my son (name)
40. Éste es mi marido (el nombre), mi hija (el nombre) y mi hijo (el nombre)

41. How long are you staying here?   41. Cuánto tiempo lleva aquí?

42. For several weeks, days, months. 42. Durante varias semanas, días, meses

43. Will you be going home?   43. Irá usted a casa?

44. Goodbye.   44. Adiós.

45. I am late.   45. Estoy tarde.

EVALUATION:
Evaluación:

46. Are you hot?   46. ¿Tiene calor?

47. I Am Hot.   47. Yo tengo calor.

48. Are you cold?   48. ¿Tiene frío?

49. I Am Cold.   49. Yo tengo frío.

50. Are you hungry?   50. ¿Tiene hambre?

51. I Am Hungry.   51. Yo tengo hambre.

52. Are you thirsty?   52. ¿Tiene sed?

53. I Am Thirsty.   53. Yo tengo sed.

54. Are you feeling good?   54. ¿Se siente bien?

55. Are you feeling sick?   55. ¿Se síente enfermo?

56. Are you feeling better?   56. ¿Se siente mejor?

57. I am feeling better now.   57. Me siento mejor ahora.

58. Are you feeling all right?   58. ¿Está usted sintiéndose bien?

59A. Do you need to use the bathroom?   59A. ¿Necesita usted usar el baño?

59B. Do you need to use the restroom?   59B. ¿Necesita usted usar los baños?

60A. I need to use the bathroom.   60A. Yo necesito usar el baño.

60B. I need to use the restroom.   60B. Yo necesito usar el baño.

61A. Where is the bathroom?   61A. ¿Dónde está el baño?

61B. Where is the restroom?   61B. ¿Dónde está el baño?

62. Here it is.

62. Aquí está.

63. Do you have pain?

63. ¿Tiene dolor?

64. I have pain.

64. Yo tengo dolor.

(See anatomy section for anatomical breakdown).
(Vea la sección de la anatomía para la avería anatómica).

65. Would you please close the window?

65. ¿Puede cerrar la ventana?

66. Would you please open the window?

66. ¿Puede abrir la ventana?

67. I am going to close the window.

67. (Yo) Voy a cerrar la ventana.

68. I am going to open the window.

68. (Yo) Voy a abrir la ventana.

69. Would you please close the door?

69. ¿Puede cerrar la puerta?

70. Would you please open the door?

70. ¿Puede abrir la puerta?

71. I am going to close the door.

71. (Yo) Voy a cerrar la puerta.

72. I am going to open the door.

72. (Yo) Voy a abrir la puerta.

73. I'll put it in the closet.

73. (Yo) lo pondré en el armario.

74. I'll put it in the drawer.

74. (Yo) lo pondré en el cajón.

75. You must take the elevator.

75. Usted debe tomar el elevador.

76. You can go up those stairs.

76. Usted puede subir esos escalones.

77. You are almost there.

77. (Usted) casi está allí.

78. You must turn around.

78. Usted debe darse la vuelta.

79. Where do you want to go?

79. Dónde usted quiere ir?

80. You are going the wrong way.

80. Usted va por dirección equivocada.

81. What time is it?

81. Qué hora es?

82. It is eight o'clock.

82. Son las ocho.

83. One

83. Uno

84. Two	84. Dos
85. Three	85. Tres
86. Four	86. Cuatro
87. Five	87. Cinco
88. Six	88. Seis
89. Seven	89. Siete
90. Eight	90. Ocho
91. Nine	91. Nueve
92. Ten	92. Diez
93. Eleven	93. Once
94. Twelve	94. Doce
95. It is noon	95. Es mediodía
96. It is midnight	96. Es media noche
97. Half past eight	97. Media hora después de las ocho.
98. Quarter before (of);	98. Un cuarto antes:
99. Quarter after	99. Un cuarto después.
100. I am an occupational therapist.	100. Yo soy un/a terapeuta ocupacional.
101. My name is Jacqueline.	101. Mi nombre es Jacqueline. OR Me llamo Jacqueline.
102. What is your name?	102. ¿Cuál es su nombre?
103. I need to see what you can do.	103. Yo necesito ver lo que usted puede hacer.
104. Do you live with family?	104. ¿Vive usted con su familia?
105. Do you live alone?	105. ¿Vive usted solo?

Anatomy:
La anatomía:

106. Head	106. Cabeza
107. Neck	107. Cuello
108. Shoulders	108. Hombros
109. Arm	109. Brazo
110. Elbow	110. Codos
111. Wrist	111. Muñeca
112. Hand	112. Mano
113. Fingers	113. Dedos
114. Chest	114. Pecho
115. Stomach/Abdomen	115. Estómago /Abdomen
116. Hips	116. Caderas
117. Buttocks	117. Trasero/Sentadera
118. Thigh	118. Muslo
119. Knee	119. Rodilla
120. Calf	120. Pantorrilla
121. Ankle	121. Tobillo
122. Foot	122. Pie
123. Toes	123. Dedos de los pies
124. Spine	124. Espina
125. Shin	125. (Espinilla) Mentón.
126. Eyes	126. Ojos
127. Ears	127. Orejas

128. Hair
128. El pelo

129. Nose
129. Nariz

130. Thumb
130. Dedo pulgar

Neuromuscular:
Neuromuscular:

131. Do you have pain?
131. ¿ Tiene usted dolor?

132. Please Show Me Where.
132. Por favor Muéstreme Dónde.

133. A little, medium, a lot?
133. ¿Un poco, mediano, mucho?

134. Can you raise your arms?
134. ¿Puede levantar sus brazos?

135. Raise your arms.
135. Levante sus brazos.

136. Lower your arms.
136. Baje sus brazos.

137. Open your hand.
137. Abra su mano.

138. Close your hand.
138. Cierre su mano.

139. Wiggle your fingers.
139. Menee sus dedos.

140. Touch your finger to your thumb.
140. Toque con su dedo pulgar.

141. Next.
141. Siguiente.

142. Squeeze my hand.
142. Apriete mi mano.

143. More, please.
143. Más, por favor.

144. Hold your arm like this.
144. Sostenga su brazo así.

145. Do not let me pull it.
145. No me permita jalarlo.

Activities of Daily Living:
Las actividades de Vivir Diariamente:

146. Which hand do you write with?
146. ¿Con qué mano escribe?

147. Which hand do you eat with?
147. ¿Con qué mano come?

148. Can you put on your clothes?

148. ¿Puede usted ponerse su ropa?

149. Can you dress yourself?

149. ¿Puedes usted vestirse?

150. Can you stand?

150. ¿Puede pararse?

Home and Community:
Casa y Comunidad:

151. Do you live in a house?

151. ¿Vive usted en una casa?

152. Do you live in an apartment?

152. ¿Vive usted en un apartamento?

153. Does someone cook for you?

153. ¿Cocina alguien para usted?

154. Does someone clean for you?

154. ¿Alguien Le limpia su casa?

155. Does someone shop (go to the market) for you, Does someone run errands for you?
155. ¿Alguien va de compras (va al mercado) por usted, alguien ejecuta los mandados por usted?

156. Does someone help you bathe?

156. ¿Le ayuda alguien a bañarse?

157. Do you have a seat in the bathtub, shower?
157. ¿Tiene usted un asiento en la bañera, la ducha?

158. Do you have a hand held shower?

158. ¿Tiene usted una doucha de mano?

159. Do you have stairs outside of your house?
159. ¿Tiene usted escalones fuera de su casa?

160. Inside?

160. ¿Dentro de?

161. How many?

161. ¿Cuántos?

162. Do you have an elevator?

162 ¿Tiene usted un elevador?

163. Are you currently working?

163. ¿Está usted trabajando actualmente?

164. Can you drive a car?

164. ¿Puede usted manejar un automóvil?

165. Can you take the bus?

165. ¿Puede usted tomar el autobús?

166. Can you do this?

166. ¿Puede usted hacer esto?

167. Do you have any questions?

167. ¿Tiene usted alguna pregunta?

TREATMENT:
El tratamiento:

168. I am an occupational therapist.   168. Yo soy un/a terapeuta ocupacional.

169. My name is Jacqueline.   169. Mi nombre es Jacqueline.
OR Me llamo Jacqueline.

170. It is time for therapy.   170. Es tiempo para la terapia.

171. It is time to eat.   171. Es hora de comer.

172. It is time to dress.   172. Es hora de vestirse.

173. It is time to exercise.   173. Es hora de hacer ejercicio.

174. Do you need to use the restroom first?   174. ¿Necesita usted usar el baño primero?

Activities of Daily Living:
Las actividades de Vivir Diariamente:

175. Would you like to bathe?   175. ¿Le gustaría bañar se?

176. Would you like to brush your teeth?   176. ¿Le gustaría cepillarse los dientes?

177. Let us brush your teeth.   177. Permítanos cepillarle sus dientes.

178. Can you do it?   178. Puede usted hacerlo?

179. I will help you.   179. Yo le ayudo.

180. Put on your shirt, pants, socks, shoes.
180. Póngase su camisa, los pantalones, los calcetines, los zapatos.

Self Feeding and Difficulty with Swallow (Dysphagia):
El mismo Alimento y Dificultad con la Golondrina (Dysphagia):

181. Pick up your fork, spoon.   181. Tome su tenedor, la cuchara.

182. Scoop your food.   182. Tome del fondo la comida.
OR reconja la comida.

183. Take a bite.   183. Dele una mordida.
OR Come un poco.

184. Swallow.   184. Tráguelo.

185. Again.

185. De nuevo.

186. Chin down.

186. Barbilla abajo.

187. Put it in your mouth.

187. Póngalo en su boca.

188. Pick up your cup, glass.

188. Tome su taza, el vaso.

189. Take a sip.

189. Tome un sorbo.

190. Drink slowly.

190. Beba despacio.

191. Just a little bit.

191. Solamente un poco.

192. Open your mouth.

192. Abra la boca.

193. Say "Ah"

193. Diga "Ah"

194. Here, take this

194. Aquí, tome esto.

195. Wipe your mouth.

195. Limpiese la boca.

Neuromuscular:
Neuromuscular:

196. Lift your arms ten times.

196. Alce sus brazos diez veces.

197. Rest.

197. Descanse.

198. Again.

198. De nuevo.

199. Pull.

199. Jale.

200. Push.

200. Empuje.

201. Turn left.

201. Doble a la izquierda.

202. Turn right.

202. Doble a la derecha.

203. On the other side.

203. Por el otro lado.

Jacqueline Thrash, OTR

Mobility:
La movilidad:

204. Sit up straight.	204. Siéntese derecho.
205. Lean forward.	205. Dóblese hacia adelante.
206. Do not lean forward.	206. No se doble hacia adelante.
207. Lean backward.	207. Doblese hacia atrás.
208. Do not lean backward.	208. No se doble hacia atrás.
209. Move forward.	209. Avance.
210. Move backward.	210. Muévase hacia atrás.
211. Put your hand here.	211. Ponga su mano aquí.
212. Right.	212. Derecho.
213. Left.	213. Izquierda.
214. Be careful.	214. Tenga cuidado.
215. Slowly.	215. Despacio.
216. Quickly.	216. Rápido.

Orientation:
La orientación:

217. What day is it?	217. ¿Qué día es?
218. What month is it?	218. ¿Qué mes es?
219. What year?	219. ¿Qué año?
220. What is your name?	220. ¿Cuál es su nombre?
221. Where are you?	221. ¿Dónde estás?
222. Why are you here?	222. ¿Por qué está aquí?
223. Are you married?	223. ¿Esta casado? (to a man) ¿Esta casada? (to a woman)

224. Do you have a husband?

224. ¿Tiene usted esposo?

225. What is your husband's name?

225. ¿Cuál es el nombre de su esposo?

226. Do you have a wife?

226. ¿Tiene usted esposa?

227. What is your wife's name?

227. ¿Cuál es el nombre de su esposa?

228. Do you have a partner?

228. ¿Tiene usted un compañero?
OR ¿Tiene usted una compañero?

229. What is his name?

229. ¿Cuál es su nombre?

230. What is her name?

230. ¿Cuál es su nombre?

231. Do you have children?

231. ¿Tiene usted hijos?

232. What are their names?

232. ¿Cómo se llaman?

233. Where do you live?

233. ¿Donde vive usted?

234. What is the season?

234. ¿Cuál es la estación?

235. Spring.

235. Primavera.

236. Summer.

236. Verano.

237. Autumn.

237. Otoño

238. Winter

238. Invierno.

239. Is it day time?

239. ¿Es de día?

240. Is it night time?

240. ¿Es de noche?

241. What time is it?

241. ¿Qué hora es?

Perception:
La percepción:

242. Blue

242. Azul

243. Red

243. Rojo

244. Yellow

244. Amarillo

245. Orange   245. Naranja

246. Green   246. Verde

247. Purple   247. Morado

248. Black   248. Negro

249. White   249. Blanco

250. Brown   250. Café.

251. Square   251. Cuadrado

252. Triangle   252. Triángulo

253. Circle   253. El círculo

254. Cube   254. El cubo

255. Draw me a picture of yourself.   255. Haga un dibujo de usted mismo.

256. Draw me a clock.   256. Dibújeme un reloj.

257. Draw me a house.   257. Dibújeme una casa.

258. Draw me a flower.   258. Dibújeme una flor.

259. Please write your name.   259. Por favor escriba su nombre.

Activities:
Las actividades:

260. Squeeze it.   260. Apriételo.

261. Pinch it.   261. Pellízquelo.

262. Pick it up.   262. Recójalo.

263. Put it down.   263. Pongalo abajo.

264. Open this, please.   264. Abra esto, por favor.

265. Close this, please.   265. Cierre esto, por favor.

266. Put it in.   266. Póngalo adentro.

267. Take it out.

267. Sáquelo.

PRECAUTIONS:
Precauciones:

Hip precautions:
Las precauciones de la cadera:

268. Do not bend more than ninety degrees.

268. No se doble más de noventa grados.

269. Keep your knees apart.

269. Separe sus rodillas.

270. Do not cross your legs.

270. No cruce las piernas.

271. Do not turn your toes inward.

271. No vuelva los dedos del pie hacia el centro.

Weight Bearing: Upper Extremities:
La presión de peso: La Extremidad Superiores:

272. Do not put weight on your arm.

272. No ponga peso en su brazo.

273. Do not put weight on your hand.

273. No ponga peso en su mano.

274. Put only a little weight.

274. Sólo ponga un poco de peso.

275. You can put more weight.

275. Puede poner más peso.

Weight Bearing: Lower Extremities:
La presión de Peso: Extremidades Inferiores:

276. Do not put weight on your foot.

276. No ponga peso en su pie.
Or Sobre su pie.

277. Only touch the floor with your toes.
277. Sólo toque el suelo con sus dedos del pie.

278. Put only a little weight.

278. Sólo ponga un poco de peso.

279. You can put more weight.

279. Ponga más peso.

Swallow Precautions:
Precauciones al tragar:

280. You must sit up for thirty minutes.
280. Usted debe sentarse por treinta minutos.

281. You can only drink thickened liquids.   281. Usted puede beber líquidos espesos.

282. Please swallow twice.   282. Traque de nuevo.

283. Please tuck your chin down.   283. Por favor baje su barbilla.

Encouragement:
El estímulo:

284. Terrific!   284. Magnífico!

285. Excellent.   285. Excelente.

286. Very Good.   286. Muy Bueno.

287. Good.   287. Bueno

288. Keep Trying.   288. Siga Intentando lo.

289. Please stop.   289. Por favor pare.

290. Hurry up, please.   290. Dése prisa, por favor.

291. We don't want to be late.   291. Nosotros no queremos llegar tarde.

292. I cannot.   292. (Yo) no puedo.

293. Yes, you can.   293. Sí, puede usted.

294. I will show you.   294. Yo le mostraré

295. Are you sure?   295. ¿ Está usted seguro?

296. That may be difficult but I will try.   296. Eso puede ser difícil pero yo lo trataré.

297. Will there be anything else?   297. ¿Habrá algo más?

298. I would be glad to.   298. Yo me alegraría de.

299. Everything is fine now.   299. Todo está ahora bien.

300. What is the matter?	300. ¿Cuál es el problema?
301. Yes, I know.	301. Sí, yo sé.
302. Yes, I could do that.	302. Sí, yo podría hacer eso.
303. I will take that.	303. Yo tomaré eso.
304. Wonderful.(perfect)	304. Maravilloso (perfecto)
305. I believe so.	305. Yo creo que sí.
306. Of course.	306. Claro. (Por supuesto)

Created by Jacqueline Thrash, OTR. Translated using L & H Power Translator Pro 7.0, Lernout & Haupie Speech Products, N.V.

Additional translation by Stephanie Meza (Mexico) and Vidal Bugarin (Mexico).

Translation verified by César Vallejo, Profesor de español, Pasadena City College.

Notes:

Notes:

Notes:

PHYSICAL THERAPY

OPENINGS AND CLOSINGS:

1. Good Morning	1. Buenos días.
2. Good Afternoon	2 Buenas tardes.
3. Good Evening	3. Buenas noches.
4. Good Night	4. Buenas noches.
5. Thank you.	5. Gracias.
6. What is your name?	6. ¿Cual es su nombre?
7. My name is Larry.	7. Mi nombre es Larry. OR Me llamo Larry.
8. Do You Speak Englísh?	8. ¿Habla usted inglés?
9. Does anyone here speak English?	9. ¿Alguien aquí habla inglés?
10. Excuse my poor Spanish.	10. Disculpe mi español.
11. I only speak a little Spanish.	11. Yo sólo hablo un poco de español.
12. I am sorry, I do not speak Spanish.	12. Lo siento, yo no hablo español.
13. Can you speak more slowly?	13. ¿Puede hablar más despacio?
14. Yes	14. Sí
15. No	15. No
16. Please	16. Por favor
17. Thanks	17. Gracias
18. Mister	18. Señor
19. Missus	19. Señora
20. Miss	20. Señorita

21. You are Welcome

21. De nada.

22. Excuse Me

22. Disculpe.

23. I Am Sorry

23. Lo Siento.

24. This is Clare.

24. Ésta es Clara.

25. How Are You?

25. ¿Cómo está usted?

26. How Have You Been?

26. ¿Cómo ha estado?

27. I am fine. Thank you.

27. Yo estoy bien. Gracias.

28. I am very glad to meet you.

28. Mucho gusto en conocerle.

29. It was nice meeting you.

29. Fue un placer conocerle.

30. What did you say?

30. ¿Qué dijo?

31. Have a nice day.

31. Que tenga un buen día.

32. That's all right.

32. Eso esta bien.

33. I understand you.

33. Yo lo entiendo. (you-male)
Yo la entiendo. (you-female)

34. I do not understand

34. Yo no entiendo.

35. I understand perfectly.

35. Yo entiendo perfectamente.

36. I understand you very well.

36. Yo lo entiendo muy bien.

37. Fine, thanks. How is your family?   37. Bien, gracias. ¿Cómo esta su familia?

38. See you later.

38. Hasta luego.

39. See you tomorrow.

39. Hasta mañana.

40. This is my husband (name), my daughter (name) and my son (name)
40. Éste es mi marido (el nombre), mi hija (el nombre) y mi hijo (el nombre)

41. How long are you staying here?   41. Cuánto tiempo lleva aquí?

42. For several weeks, days, months.   42. Durante varias semanas, días, meses

43. Will you be going home?   43. Irá usted a casa?

44. Goodbye.   44. Adiós.

45. I am late.   45. Estoy tarde.

EVALUATION:
Evaluación:

46. Are you hot?   46. ¿Tiene calor?

47. I Am Hot.   47. Yo tengo calor.

48. Are you cold?   48. ¿Tiene frío?

49. I Am Cold.   49. Yo tengo frío.

50. Are you hungry?   50. ¿Tiene hambre?

51. I Am Hungry.   51. Yo tengo hambre.

52. Are you thirsty?   52. ¿Tiene sed?

53. I Am Thirsty.   53. Yo tengo sed.

54. Are you feeling good?   54. ¿Se siente bien?

55. Are you feeling sick?   55. ¿Se síente enfermo?

56. Are you feeling better?   56. ¿Se siente mejor?

57. I am feeling better now.   57. Me siento mejor ahora.

58. Are you feeling all right?   58. ¿Está usted sintiéndose bien?

59A. Do you need to use the bathroom?   59A. ¿Necesita usted usar el baño?

59B. Do you need to use the restroom?   59B. ¿Necesita usted usar los baños?

60A. I need to use the bathroom.   60A. Yo necesito usar el baño.

60B. I need to use the restroom.   60B. Yo necesito usar el baño.

61A. Where is the bathroom?   61A. ¿Dónde está el baño?

61B. Where is the restroom?   61B. ¿Dónde está el baño?

62. Here it is.

62. Aquí está.

63. Do you have pain?

63. ¿Tiene dolor?

64. I have pain.

64. Yo tengo dolor.

(See anatomy section for anatomical breakdown).
(Vea la sección de la anatomía para la avería anatómica).

65. Would you please close the window?

65. ¿Puede cerrar la ventana?

66. Would you please open the window?

66. ¿Puede abrir la ventana?

67. I am going to close the window.

67. (Yo) Voy a cerrar la ventana.

68. I am going to open the window.

68. (Yo) Voy a abrir la ventana.

69. Would you please close the door?

69. ¿Puede cerrar la puerta?

70. Would you please open the door?

70. ¿Puede abrir la puerta?

71. I am going to close the door.

71. (Yo) Voy a cerrar la puerta.

72. I am going to open the door.

72. (Yo) Voy a abrir la puerta.

73. I'll put it in the closet.

73. (Yo) lo pondré en el armario.

74. I'll put it in the drawer.

74. (Yo) lo pondré en el cajón.

75. You must take the elevator.

75. Usted debe tomar el elevador.

76. You can go up those stairs.

76. Usted puede subir esos escalones.

77. You are almost there.

77. (Usted) casi está allí.

78. You must turn around.

78. Usted debe darse la vuelta.

79. Where do you want to go?

79. Dónde usted quiere ir?

80. You are going the wrong way.

80. Usted va por dirección equivocada.

81. What time is it?

81. Qué hora es?

82. It is eight o'clock.

82. Son las ocho.

83. One

83. Uno

84. Two	84. Dos
85. Three	85. Tres
86. Four	86. Cuatro
87. Five	87. Cinco
88. Six	88. Seis
89. Seven	89. Siete
90. Eight	90. Ocho
91. Nine	91. Nueve
92. Ten	92. Diez
93. Eleven	93. Once
94. Twelve	94. Doce
95. It is noon	95. Es mediodía
96. It is midnight	96. Es media noche
97. Half past eight	97. Media hora después de las ocho.
98. Quarter before (of);	98. Un cuarto antes:
99. Quarter after	99. Un cuarto después.
100. I am a physical therapist.	100. Soy un fisicio-terapeuta.
101. My name is Larry.	101. Mi nombre es Larry. OR Me llamo Larry.
102. What is your name?	102. ¿Cual es su nombre?
103. I need to see how you can move.	103. Necesito ver cómo se puede mover.
104. I need to see how you can walk.	104. Necesito ver cómo puede caminar.
105. Are you ready?	105. ¿Listo?
106. Do you need to dress?	106. ¿Necesita vestirse?

107. Do you need the nurse?   107. ¿Necesita la enfermera?

108. Can you move your legs?   108. ¿Puede mover sus piernas?

109. Can you stand?   109. ¿Puede ponerse de pie?

110. Can you walk?   110. ¿Puede caminar?

111. Do you need to use the restroom, first?   111. ¿Necesita usted usar el baño primero?

112A. Do you need a wheelchair?   112A. ¿Necesita una silla de ruedas?

113A. I will get you a wheelchair.   113A. Voy a conseguir le silla de ruedas.

112B. Do you need a walker?   112B. ¿Necesita un caminador?

113B. I will get you a walker.   113B. Voy a conseguir un caminador.

Anatomy:
La anatomía:

114. Head   114. Cabeza

115. Neck   115. Cuello

116. Shoulders   116. Hombros

117. Arm   117. Brazo

118. Elbow   118. Codos

119. Wrist   119. Muñeca

120. Hand   120. Mano

121. Fingers   121. Dedos

122. Chest   122. Pecho

123. Stomach/Abdomen   123. Estómago /Abdomen

124. Hips   124. Caderas

125. Buttocks   125. Trasero/Sentadera

126. Thigh/Leg   126. Muslo/Pierna

127. Knee	127. Rodilla
128. Calf	128. Pantorrilla
129. Ankle	129. Tobillo
130. Foot	130. Pie
131. Toes	131. Dedos del pies
132. Spine	132. Espina
133. Shin	133. Espinilla
134. Eyes	134. Ojos
135. Ears	135. Orejas
136. Hair	136. El pelo
137. Nose	137. Nariz
138. Thumb	138. Dedo pulgar

Neuromuscular:
Neuromuscular:

139. Raise your right leg.	139. Levánte su pierna derecha.
140. Raise your left leg.	140. Levánte su pierna izquierda.
141. Bend your knee.	141. Doble la rodilla.
142. Straighten your knee.	142. Enderece la rodilla.
143. Bend your hip.	143. Doble la cadera.
144. Straighten your hip.	144. Enderece la cadera.
145. Keep your leg bent.	145. Mantenga la pierna doblado.
146. Keep your leg straight.	146. Mantenga derecha la pierna.
147. Hold it.	147. Deténgase.
148. Kick out your right foot.	148. Levánte el pie derecho.

149. Kick out your left foot.

149. Levánte el pie izquierdo.

150. Wiggle your toes.

150. Mueva los dedos del los pies.

151. Bring your toes up.

151. Levánte los dedos del los pies.

152. Point your toes.

152. Apunte hacia arriba los dedos de los pies.

Sensation:
Sensación:

153. Can you feel this?

153. ¿Siente usted esto?

154. Here?

154. ¿Aquí?

155. And Here?

155. ¿Y aquí?

156. Is it sharp?

156. ¿Lo siente agudo?

157. Is it dull?

157. ¿No esta agudo?

158. Is it hot?

158. ¿Está caliente?
OR ¿Siente calor?

159. Is it cold?

159. ¿Esta frió?

Prosthetics:
Próstesis:

160. Do you have a prosthetic (artificial leg)?

160. ¿Tiene una pierna postiza?

161. Does it cause redness.

161. ¿Le causa irritación?

162. Does it cause blisters?

162. ¿Esto le causa ampollas?

163. Is it too tight?

163. ¿Este muy apretado/a?

164. Is it too loose?

164. ¿Este muy suelto/a?

165. May I look at your leg?

165. Por favor, permitame mirar su pierna.

166. I am going to measure your leg.

166. Voy a medir le/la pierna.

167. May I look at your knee?

167. Permitame mirarle le/la rodilla?

168. Can you straighten your knee?

168. ¿Puede enderezar la rodilla?

169. Your knee must be straight in order to walk.
169. Su rodilla necesita estar recto por caminar.
OR Debe mantener la rodilla derecha para poder caminar.

170. We will get you a prosthetic (artificial leg).
170. Le conseguiremos una pierna postiza.

171. I am going to call the prosthetist.

171. Voy a llamar al prosteitista/o.

172. He/she will make you a new leg.

172. El/ella le hará una pierna nueva.

173. I will teach you exercises to make your leg stronger.
173. Le enseñaré algunos ejercicios para darle mas fuerza a la pierna.

Mobility:
La movilidad:

174. Scoot forward.

174. Córrase hacia adelante.

175. Scoot backward.

175. Córrase atrás.

176. Put your hand here.

176. Ponga la mano aquí.

177. Reach back more.

177. Estirela más, hacia atrás.

178. Lean forward.

178. Inclínese hacia adelante.

179. Lean backward.

179. Inclínese hacia atrás.

180. Do not fall backward

180. No se caiga hacia atrás.

181. Push off the bed.

181. Empújese fuera de la cama.

182. Push off the chair.

182. Empuje la silla.

183. Stand up.

183. Párese
OR Póngase de pie.

184. Sit down

184. Siéntese.

185. Put your hand on the armrest.

185. Ponga la mano sobre brazo de la silla.

186. Put your hand on the wheelchair.

186. Ponga la mano sobre la silla de ruedas.

Wheelchair Mobility:
La Movilidad de la Silla de Ruedas:

187. Lock the wheelchair brakes.

187. Ponga los frenos de la silla de ruedas.

188. Unlock the wheelchair brakes.

188. Quite los frenos de la silla de ruedas.

189. Push on the wheels.

189. Empuje las ruedas.
OR Mueva las ruedas.

190. Push more with your right hand.

190. Empújese mas con su mano derecha.

191. Push more with your left hand.

191. Empújese mas con su mano izquierda.

192. Go straight ahead.

192. Vaya derecho.

193. Turn right.

193. Dé una vuelta a la derecha.

194. Turn left.

194. Dé una vuelta a la izquierda.

195. Turn around and go back.

195. Dé una vuelta y devuélvase.

Ambulation:
Al Caminar:

196. Let me help you sit up.

196. Déjeme ayudarle a sentarse.

197. Let me put this belt around your waist.
197. Déjame ponerle este cinturón alrededor de la cintura.

198. Ready?

198. ¿Listo?

199. Scoot forward.

199. Córrase hacia adelante.

200. Push with your hands.

200. Empújese con las manos.

201. Stand up.

201. Levántese.

202A. Put your right hand here.

202A. Póngase la mano izquierda aquí.

202B. Put your left hand here.

202B. Póngase la mano derecha aquí.

203. This is a walker.

203. Este es un caminador.

204. Move walker forward.

204. Mueva el caminador hacia adelante.

205A. Step forward with your right leg.
205A. Dé un paso adelante con la pierna derecha.

205B. Step forward with your left leg.
205B. Dé un paso adelante con la pierna izquierda.

206. Bring your other leg forward.

206. Traiga la otra pierna adelante.
OR Mueva la otra pierna hacia adelante.

207. Move walker forward, again.

207. Mueva el caminador hacia adelante, otra vez.

208. Take a step forward.

208. Dé un paso adelante.

209. Take a step backward.

209. Dé un paso hacia atrás.

210. Do not put weight on your right foot.

210. No ponga peso en el pie derecho.
OR No se apoye mucho en el pie derecho.

211. Do not put weight on your left foot.

211. No ponga peso en el pie izquierdo.
OR No se apoye mucho en el pie izquierdo.

212. You can put weight on your right foot.

212. Puedes poner peso en el pie derecha.
OR Puede apoyarse en el pie derecho.

213. You can put weight on your left foot.

213. Puedes poner peso en el pie izquierdo.
OR Puede apoyarse en el pie izquierdo.

214. More weight.

214. Más peso.

215. Less weight.

215. Menos peso.

216. Are you tired?

216. ¿Está cansado/a?

217. Just a little more.

217. ¡Un poquito más!

218. Then you can sit down.

218. Pues puede sentarse.

219. Can you go further?

219. ¿Puede ir un poco más adelante?

220. Are you dizzy?

220. ¿Está mareado?

221. Okay.

221. Vale.

222. I will help you sit down.

222. Puedo ayudarle a sentarse.

223. Step backwards.

223.Un paso hacia atrás.

224. Reach back with your hand.

224. Tóquese la espalda con la mano.

225. Can you feel the chair with your legs?

225. ¿Puedes sentir la silla con las piernas?

226. Sit down.

226. Siéntese.

227. Scoot backwards.

227. Córrase atrás.

Home and Community:
Casa y Comunidad:

228. Do you live in a house?

228. ¿Vive en una casa?

229. Do you live in an apartment?

229. ¿Vive en una apartamente?

230. Do you live alone?

230. ¿Habita solo?

231. Do you live with someone?

231. ¿Habita con un otro?

232. Husband.

232. Esposo.

233. Wife.

233. Esposa.

234. Friend.

234. Amigo/Amiga.

235. Partner (gay)

235. Compañero/a

236. Roommate.

236. Compañero de cuarto.

237. Son.

237. Hijo.

238. Daughter.

238. Hija.

239. Grandson.

239. Nieto.

240. Granddaughter.

240. Nieta.

241A. Do you have stairs inside?

241A. ¿Tiene escalones gradas/duentro de la casa?

241B. Do you have stairs outside?

241B. ¿Tiene escalones afuera?

242. How many?

242. ¿Cuánto(s)?

243. Do you have an elevator?

243. ¿Tiene un ascensor?

244. Do you have a ramp?

244. ¿Tiene una rampa?

245. Do you have a wheelchair at home?

245. ¿Tiene una silla de ruedas en su casa?

246. Do you have a walker at home?

246. ¿Tiene una andadera en su casa?

247. Do you have a cane at home?

247. ¿Tiene una bastón en su casa?

248. Do you have a tub?

248. ¿Tiene una bañera?

249. Do you have a shower?

249. ¿Tiene una ducha?

250. Do you have a seat in your tub, shower?
250. ¿Tiene una silla en su bañera, ducha?

251. Do have bars in your tub, shower?
251. ¿Tiene las barras de mano en su bañera, ducha?

252. Can you drive a car?

252. ¿Puedes conducir un automóvil?

253. Can you take the bus?

253. ¿Puede tomar el autobús?

TREATMENT:
Tratamiento:

254. My name is Larry.

254. Mi nombre es Larry.
OR Me llamo Larry.

255. I am the physical therapist.

255. Soy un fisicio-terapeuta.

256. It is time for therapy.

256. Ésta la hora para terapia.

257. It is time to exercise.

257. Ésta la hora para ejercisio.

258. It is time to walk.

258. Ésta es la hora para caminar.

259. Do you need to use the restroom first?
259. ¿Necesita usted usar el baño primero?

Neuromuscular:
Neuromuscular:

260. Raise your right leg.

260. Levánte su pierna derecha.

261. Raise your left leg.

261. Levánte su pierna izquierda.

262. Bend your knee.

262. Doble la rodilla.

263. Straighten your knee.	263. Enderece la rodilla.
264. Bend your hip.	264. Doble la cadera.
265. Straighten your hip.	265. Enderece la cadera.
266. Keep your leg bent.	266. Mantenga la pierna doblado.
267. Keep your leg straight.	267. Mantenga derecha la pierna.
268. Hold it.	268. Deténgase.
269. Kick out your right foot.	269. Levánte el pie derecho.
270. Kick out your left foot.	270. Levánte el pie izquierdo.
271. Wiggle your toes.	271. Mueva los dedos del los pies.
272. Bring your toes up.	272. Levánte los dedos del los pies.
273. Point your toes.	273. Apunte hacia arribe los dedos del los pies.
274. Lift your right leg ten times.	274. Levantese la pierna derecha diez veces.
275. Rest.	275. Descanse.
276. Repeat.	276. Repita.
277. Now, the left leg.	277. Ahora, la pierna izguierda.
278. Kick your foot out ten times.	278. Estire el pie diez veces.
279. Bring your knee up ten times.	279. Levante la rodilla diez veces.

Prosthetics:
Próstesis:

280. This is a stump wrap.	280. Éste es el envoltorio de un munón.
281. It will help make your leg smaller.	281. Le ayuda a tener la pierna más corta OR Le ayuda a encogir la pierna.
282. Then we can fit your new leg.	282. Ahora podemos ajustarle la pierna nueva.
283. This is a stump shrinker.	283. Esto encoje el munón.

284. It will also make your leg smaller.

284. Esto encoge más la pierna.

285. This is a stump sock.

285. Este es calcetín del (un) munón.

286. It will pad your stump.

286. Esto acolchona el munón.

287. This is a belt.

287. Éste es un cinto.

288. It will help secure your artificial leg.

288. Le ayuda a sujetar su pierna postiza.

289. This is how you put it on.

289. Así es cómo se lo debe poner.

290. Please put it on.

290. Por favor póngaselo/la.

291. This is how you put on your stump shrinker.
291. Esto es cómo se jone el encogedor del munón.

292. This is how you put on your stump sock.
292. Así es cómo debe ponerse el calcetín del munón.

293. Please put it on.

293. Por favor póngase lo.

294. Please put on another.

294. Por favor póngase uno mas.

295. Make sure it is smooth.

295. Asegeírese que esté suave/liso.

296. No wrinkles.

296. Sin arrugas.

297. No creases.

297. Sin arrugas.

298. Put your stump into the artificial leg opening.
298. Póngase el munón en la apertura de la pierna postiza.

299. Put it on firmly.

299. Póngase lo firmemente.

300. Please fasten the belt.

300. Por favor abróchese el cinturón/cinto.
OR Por favor amárrese el cinturón/cinto.

301. Put your trousers (pants) over the artificial leg.
301. Ponga los pantalones por encima de la pierna postiza.

302. Put your other leg into your pants.

302. Ponga la otra pierna en los pantalones.

303. Pull your trousers (pants) over your hips.
303. Tire los pantalones abrededor de la cintura.

304. Fasten your trousers (pants).

304. Sujétese su pantalones.

305. You can do it lying down.

305. Se los puede joner acostado.

306. You can do it sitting at the edge of the bed.
306. Lo puede hacei sentado al borde de la cama.

Mobility:
La movilidad:

307. Let me help you sit up.

307. Déjeme ayudarle a sentarse.

308. Let me help you get out of bed.

308. Permitame ayudar le a levantanse de la cama.

309. Let me help you stand.

309. Permitame ayudar le a ponerse de pie.

310. Sit up here.

310. Siéntese aquí.

311. Scoot up in bed.

311. Córrase arriba en la cama.

312. Scoot down in bed.

312. Póngase abajo en la cama.

313. Scoot left.

313. Córrase a le izquierda.

314. Scoot right.

314. Córrase a le derecha.

315. Scoot forward.

315. Córrase hacia adelante.

316. Scoot backward.

316. Córrase atrás.

317. Put your hand here.

317. Ponga la mano aquí.

318. Reach back more.

318. Estirela más, hacia atrás.

319. Lean forward.

319. Inclínese hacia adelante.

320. Lean backward.

320. Inclínese hacia atrás.

321. Do not fall backward.

321. No se caiga hacia atrás.

322. Stand up.

322. Párese
OR Póngase de pie.

323. Sit down.

323. Siéntese.

324. Push off the bed.

324. Empújese fuera de la cama.

325. Push off the chair.

325. Empuje la silla.

326. Put your hand on the armrest.

326. Ponga la mano sobre el brazo de la silla.

327. Put your hand on the wheelchair.

327. Ponga la mano sobre la silla de ruedas.

Wheelchair Mobility:
La Movilidad de la Silla de Ruedas:

328. Lock the wheelchair brakes.

328. Ponga los frenos de la silla de ruedas.

329. Unlock the wheelchair brakes.

329. Quite los frenos de la silla de ruedas.

330. Push on the wheels.

330. Empuje las ruedas.
OR Mueva las ruedas.

331. Push more with your right hand.

331. Empújese mas con su mano derecha.

332. Push more with your left hand.

332. Empújese mas con su mano izquierda.

333. Go straight ahead.

333. Vaya derecho.

334. Turn right.

334. Dé una vuelta a la derecha.

335. Turn left.

335. Dé una vuelta a la izquierda.

336. Turn around and go back.

336. Dé una vuelta y devuélvase.

Ambulation:
Al Caminar:

337. Let me put this belt around your waist.
337. Déjame ponerle este cinturón alrededor de la cintura.

338. Ready?

338. ¿Listo?

339. Scoot forward.

339. Córrase hacia adelante.

340. Push with your hands.

340. Empújese con sus manos.

341. Stand up.

341. Párese OR
Póngase de pie.

342. Put your right hand here.

342. Póngase la mano izquierda aquí.

343. Put your left hand here.

343. Póngase la mano derecha aquí.

344. Move walker forward.

344. Mueva el caminador hacia adelante.

345A. Step forward with your right leg.
345A. Dé un paso adelante con la pierna derecha.

345B. Step forward with your left leg.
345B. Dé un paso adelante con la pierna izquierda.

346. Bring your other forward.

346. Traiga su otra pierna adelante.
OR Estire su otra pierna adelante.

347. Move walker forward, again.

347. Mueva el caminador hacia adelante de muero.

348A. Step forward with your left leg.
348A. Dé un paso adelante con la pierna izquierda.

348B. Step forward with your right leg.
348B. Dé un paso adelante con la pierna derecha.

349A. Bring your right leg forward.

349A. Estire la pierna derecha adelante.

349B. Bring your left leg forward.

349B. Estire la pierna izquierda adelante.

350. Move walker forward, again.

350. Mueva el caminador hacia adelante, otra vez.

351A. Take a step forward.

351A. Dé un paso adelante.

351B. Take a step backward.

351B. Dé un paso hacia atrás.

352A. Do not put weight on your right foot.

352A. No ponga peso en el pie derecho.
OR No se apoye mucho en el pie derecho.

352B. Do not put weight on your left foot.

352B. No ponga peso en el pie izquierdo.
OR No se apoye mucho en el pie izquierdo.

353A. You can put weight on your right foot.

353A. Puede poner peso en el pie derecha.
OR Puede apoyarse en el pie derecho.

353B. You can put weight on your left foot.

353B. Puedes poner peso en el pie izquierdo
OR Puede apoyarse en el pie izquierdo.

354. More weight.

354. Más peso.

355. Less weight.

355. Menos peso.

356. Are you tired?

356. ¿ Cansado/a?

357. Just a little more.

357. ¡Un poquito más!

358. Then you can sit down.

358. Pues puede sentarse.

359. Can you go further?

359. ¿Puede ir un poco más adelante?

360. Are you dizzy?

360. ¿Está mareado?

361. Okay.

361. Vale.

362. I will help you sit down.

362. Puedo ayudarle a sentarse.

363. Step backwards.

363. Un paso hacia atrás.

364. Reach back with your hand.

364. Tóquese la espalda con la mano.

365. Can you feel the chair with your legs?   365. ¿Puedes sentir la silla con las piernas?

366. Sit down.

366. Siéntese.

367. Scoot backwards.

367. Córrase atrás.

Gross Motor Skills:
Entrenamento Para Los Músculos Grandes:

Ball Toss:
Sacudir Pelota:

368. Take the ball.

368. Tome la pelota.

369. Use two hands.

369. Use las dos manos.

370. Use your right hand.

370. Use la mano derecha.

371. Use your left hand.

371. Use la mano izquierda.

372. Hold it here.

372. Deténgase aquí.

373. Throw it to me.

373. Tíremela.

374. Catch the ball.

374. Agarre la pelota.
OR Tome la pelota.

375. Try again.

375. Pruebe.

Ring Toss:
Sacudir el anillo:

376. Take the ring.	376. Tome el anilla.
377. Hold it like this.	377. Sujételo así.
378. Reach back.	378. Llevelo hacia atrás.
379. Bring your hand forward.	379. Estire la mano adelante.
380. Let go.	380. Dejelo ir.

Ball Kicking:
Patear la pelota.

381. Are you ready?	381. ¿Listo?
382. Here it comes.	382. ¡Ahora! ¡Dele! ¡Vamos!
383. Kick it with your right foot.	383. Dele una patada con el pie derecho.
384. Kick it with your left foot.	384. Dele una patada con el pie izquierda.
385. Try again.	385. Pruebe.

Seated Exercises:
Ejercicio en la silla:

Upper Extremities:
Extremidades Superiores:

386. Put your hands over your head.	386. Póngase las manos en la cabeza.
387. Put your arms like this.	387. Ponga los brazos así.
388. Reach for the ceiling.	388. Estírse hacia arriba. OR Estire los brazos hacia arriba.
389. Hold it.	389. Deténgase.
390. Bring your hands down.	390. Baje los manos.
391. Put your arms in front.	391. Pongase los brazos hacia el frente.
392. Palms up.	392. Palmas arriba.

393. Palms down.

393. Palmas abajo.

394. Do it ten times.

394. Hágalo diez veces.

395. Spread your fingers.

395. Estire los dedos.

396. Make a fist.

396. Empune la mano.
OR Haga un puno.

397. Again.

397. Otra vez.

398. Keep your elbows straight.

398. Mantenga el codo estirado.

399. Bend one elbow.

399. Doble el codo.

400. Bend the other one.

400. Doble el otro.

401. Alternate.

401. Alterne.

402. Like this.

402. ¡Así!

403. Do it ten times.

403. Hágalo diez veces.

404. Bring your arms to the side, like this.

404. Estire los brazos al lad, así.

405. Down.

405. Bájelos.

406. Up.

406. Levántelo (hacia arriba).

407. Do it ten times.

407. Hágalo diez veces.

Lower Extremities:
Extremidades Inferiores:

408. Straighten your leg.

408. Estire la pierna.

409A. Put your right foot out in front.

409A. Estire el pie derecho hacia el frente.

409B. Put your right foot back.

409B. Ponga el pie derecho normal.

410A. Put your left foot out in front.

410A. Estire el pie izquierdo hacia el frente.

410B. Put your left foot back.

410B. Devuelva el pie izquierdo

411A. Point your toes down

411A. Estire los dedos del pies hacia abajo.
OR Ponga los dedos del pies hacia abajo.

411B. Point your toes up.

411B. Ponga los dedos del pies hacia arriba.

412A. Turn your ankle to the right.

412A. Voltee el tobillo a la derecha.

412B. Turn your ankle to the left.

412B. Voltee el tobillo a la izquierdo

413. Bend your leg.

413. Doble le pierna.

414A. Lift your knee up.

414A. Levante la rodilla hacia arriba.

414B. Put it down.

414B. Bájela.

415. Now the other one.

415. Ahora la otra.

416. March in place.

416. Marche ahí mismo.

417. Bring your knees apart.

417. Separe los rodillas.

418. Bring your knees together.

418. Ponga las rodillos juntas.
OR Junte las rodillas.

PRECAUTIONS:
PRECAUCIONES:

Hip Precautions:
Las precauciones de la cadera:

419. Do not bend more than ninety degrees.

419. No se doble más de noventa grados.

420. Keep your knees apart.

420. Separe sus rodillas.

421. Do not cross your legs.

421. No cruce las piernas.

422. Do not turn your toes inward.

422. No vuelva los dedos del pie hacia el centro.

Weight Bearing: Upper Extremities:
La presión de peso: Extremidades Superiores:

423. Do not put weight on your arm.

423. No le ponga mucho peso en el brazo.

424. Do not put weight on your hand.

424. No le ponga peso a le mano.

425. Put only a little weight.

425. Póngale un poco de peso, no más.

426. You can put more weight.

426. Puede ponerle más peso.

Weight Bearing: Lower Extremities:
La Presión de peso: Extremidades Inferiores:

427. Do not put weight on your right foot.   427. No le ponga peso al pie derecho.

428. Do not put weight on your left foot.   428. No le ponga peso al pie izquierdo.

429. Only touch the floor with your toes.
429. Toque solamente el piso con los dedos de los pies.

430. Lift up your heel.   430. Levante el talon.

431. Put only a little weight on your right foot
431. Póngale un poco de peso al pie derecho.

432. Put only a little weight on your left foot.
432. Póngale un poco de peso al pie izquierdo.

433. You can put more weight.   433. Póngale más peso.
OR Puede ponerle más peso.
OR Puede hacerle más peso.

Swallow Precautions:
Precauciones al tragar:

434. You must sit up for thirty minutes.
434. Usted debe sentarse por treinta minutos.

435. The speech therapist said you can only drink thickened liquids.
435. La terapeuta del habla dijo que solamente puede tomar (beber) líquidos espesos.

Encouragement:
El estímulo:

436. Step by step.   436. Paso a paso.

437. Little by little.   437. Poco a poco.

438. Terrific!   438. Terrífico!

439. Excellent.   439. Excelente.

440. Very Good.   440. Muy Bueno.

441. Good.   441. Bueno.

442. Keep Trying.   442. Siga Intentando lo.

443. Please stop.

443. Por favor pare.

444. Hurry up, please.

444. Dése prisa, por favor.

445. We don't want to be late.

445. Nosotros no queremos llegar tarde.

446. I cannot.

446.(Yo) no puedo.

447. Yes, you can.

447. Sí, (usted) puedes.

448. I will show you.

448. Yo le mostraré.

449. Are you sure?

449. ¿ Está usted seguro?

450. That may be difficult but I will try.

450. Eso puede ser difícil pero yo lo trataré.

451. Will there be anything else?

451. ¿Habrá algo más?

452. I would be glad to.

452. Yo me alegraría de.

453. Everything is fine now.

453. Todo está ahora bien.

454. What is the matter?

454. Cuál es la problema?

455. Yes, I know.

455. Sí, yo sé.

456. Yes, I could do that.

456. Sí, yo podría hacer eso.

457. I will take that.

457. Yo tomaré eso.

458.Wonderful.(perfect)

458.Maravilloso (perfecto)

459. I believe so.

459. Yo creo ane si.

460. Of course.

460. Claro. (Por supuesto)

PT Phrases created by Jacqueline Thrash, OTR, and Lucy Escobar, PTA.
Verified by: Roger Williams, PhD, RPT, University of Puget Sound.

Translations by: Jacqueline Thrash, OTR.
Additional translations by Stephanie Meza (Mexico) and Vidal Bugarin (Mexico).

Translations verified by Profesor of español, César J. Vallejo, Pasadena City College.

Notes:

Notes:

SPEECH THERAPY

ST ENGLISH TO SPANISH (LATIN) by Jacqueline Thrash, OTR © **2006**

OPENINGS AND CLOSINGS:

1. Good Morning	1. Buenos días.
2. Good Afternoon	2 Buenas tardes.
3. Good Evening	3. Buenas noches.
4. Good Night	4. Buenas noches.
5. Thank you.	5. Gracias.
6. What is your name?	6. ¿Cual es su nombre?
7. My name is Reshmi.	7. Mi nombre es Reshmi. OR Me llamo Reshmi.
8. Do You Speak English?	8. ¿Habla usted inglés?
9. Does anyone here speak English?	9. ¿Alguien aquí habla inglés?
10. Excuse my poor Spanish.	10. Disculpe mi español.
11. I only speak a little Spanish.	11. Yo sólo hablo un poco de español.
12. I am sorry, I do not speak Spanish.	12. Lo siento, yo no hablo español.
13. Can you speak more slowly?	13. ¿Puede hablar más despacio?
14. Yes	14. Sí
15. No	15. No
16. Please	16. Por favor
17. Thanks	17. Gracias
18. Mister	18. Señor
19. Missus	19. Señora
20. Miss	20. Señorita

21. You are Welcome

21. De nada.

22. Excuse Me

22. Disculpe.

23. I Am Sorry

23. Lo Siento.

24. This is Clare.

24. Ésta es Clara.

25. How Are You?

25. ¿Cómo está usted?

26. How Have You Been?

26. ¿Cómo ha estado?

27. I am fine. Thank you.

27. Yo estoy bien. Gracias.

28. I am very glad to meet you.

28. Mucho gusto en conocerle.

29. It was nice meeting you.

29. Fue un placer conocerle.

30. What did you say?

30. ¿Qué dijo?

31. Have a nice day.

31. Que tenga un buen día.

32. That's all right.

32. Eso esta bien.

33. I understand you.

33. Yo lo entiendo. (you-male)
    Yo la entiendo. (you-female)

34. I do not understand

34. Yo no entiendo

35. I understand perfectly.

35. Yo entiendo perfectamente.

36. I understand you very well.

36. Yo lo entiendo muy bien.

37. Fine, thanks. How is your family?

37. Bien, gracias. ¿Cómo esta su familia?

38. See you later.

38. Hasta luego.

39. See you tomorrow.

39. Hasta mañana.

40. This is my husband (name), my daughter (name) and my son (name)
40. Éste es mi marido (el nombre), mi hija (el nombre) y mi hijo (el nombre)

41. How long are you staying here?   41. Cuánto tiempo lleva aquí?

42. For several weeks, days, months.   42. Durante varias semanas, días, meses

43. Will you be going home?   43. Irá usted a casa?

44. Goodbye.   44. Adiós.

45. I am late.   45. Estoy tarde.

EVALUATION:
Evaluación:

46. Are you hot?   46. ¿Tiene calor?

47. I Am Hot.   47. Yo tengo calor.

48. Are you cold?   48. ¿Tiene frío?

49. I Am Cold.   49. Yo tengo frío.

50. Are you hungry?   50. ¿Tiene hambre?

51. I Am Hungry.   51. Yo tengo hambre.

52. Are you thirsty?   52. ¿Tiene sed?

53. I Am Thirsty.   53. Yo tengo sed.

54. Are you feeling good?   54. ¿Se siente bien?

55. Are you feeling sick?   55. ¿Se síente enfermo?

56. Are you feeling better?   56. ¿Se siente mejor?

57. I am feeling better now.   57. Me siento mejor ahora.

58. Are you feeling all right?   58. ¿Está usted sintiéndose bien?

59A. Do you need to use the bathroom?   59A. ¿Necesita usted usar el baño?

59B. Do you need to use the restroom?   59B. ¿Necesita usted usar los baños?

60A. I need to use the bathroom.   60A. Yo necesito usar el baño.

60B. I need to use the restroom.   60B. Yo necesito usar el baño.

61A. Where is the bathroom?   61A. ¿Dónde está el baño?

61B. Where is the restroom?   61B. ¿Dónde está el baño?

62. Here it is.   62. Aquí está.

63. Do you have pain?   63. ¿Tiene dolor?

64. I have pain.   64. Yo tengo dolor.

65. Would you please close the window?   65. ¿Puede cerrar la ventana?

66. Would you please open the window?   66. ¿Puede abrir la ventana?

67. I am going to close the window.   67. (Yo) Voy a cerrar la ventana.

68. I am going to open the window.   68. (Yo) Voy a abrir la ventana.

69. Would you please close the door?   69. ¿Puede cerrar la puerta?

70. Would you please open the door?   70. ¿Puede abrir la puerta?

71. I am going to close the door.   71. (Yo) Voy a cerrar la puerta.

72. I am going to open the door.   72. (Yo) Voy a abrir la puerta.

73. I'll put it in the closet.   73. (Yo) lo pondré en el armario.

74. I'll put it in the drawer.   74. (Yo) lo pondré en el cajón.

75. You must take the elevator.   75. Usted debe tomar el elevador.

76. You can go up those stairs.   76. Usted puede subir esos escalones.

77. You are almost there.   77. (Usted) casi está allí.

78. You must turn around.   78. Usted debe darse la vuelta.

79. Where do you want to go?   79. Dónde usted quiere ir?

80. You are going the wrong way.   80. Usted va por dirección equivocada..

81. What time is it?   81. Qué hora es?

82. It is eight o'clock.   82. Son las ocho.

83. One	83. Uno
84. Two	84.Dos
85. Three	85. Tres
86. Four	86. Cuatro
87. Five	87. Cinco
88. Six	88. Seis
89. Seven	89. Siete
90. Eight	90. Ocho
91. Nine	91. Nueve
92. Ten	92. Diez
93. Eleven	93. Once
94. Twelve	94. Doce
95. It is noon	95. Es mediodía
96. It is midnight	96. Es media noche
97. Half past eight	97. Media hora después de las ocho.
98. Quarter before (of);	98. Un cuarto antes:
99. Quarter after	99. Un cuarto después.

Swallow Evaluation and Treatment:
Evaluación y Tratamiento en el Tragar:

100. I am a speech therapist.	100. Yo soy una terapista de habla.
101. My name is Reshmi.	101. Mi nombre es Reshmi. OR Me llamo Reshmi.
102. What is your name?	102. ¿Cuál es su nombre?

103. I need to evaluate your ability to swallow.
103. Yo necisito evaluar su habilidad de tragar.

104. I am going to give you something to eat and drink.
104. Yo voy a darle algo de comer y beber.

105. Take a bite.

106. Take a sip.

107. Open your mouth.

108. Put your tongue out.

109. Put your tongue in.

110. Move your tongue side to side.

111. Move your tongue up.

112. Pucker your lips.

113. Retract your lips (smile).

114. Say "Ah".

115. Close your mouth.

116. Swallow.

117. Swallow again.

118. Cough.

119. Clear your throat.

120. Lick your lips.

121. Take small bites.

122. Take small sips.

123. Tuck your chin down.

124. Does it hurt?

125. Is it hard to swallow?

105. Tome una traquito.
OR Tome un pedicito.

106. Tome un sorbo.

107. Abra su boca.

108. Saque su lengua.

109. Meta le lengua.

110. Mueva su lengua de lado-a lado.

111. Suba su lengua.

112. Ponga su labios de piquito.

113. Ponga los labios normales (sonria)

114. Diga "Ah".

115. Cierre su boca.

116. Pasatelo.

117. Trague de nuevo.

118. Tosa

119. Limpie su garganta.

120. Lama sus labios.

121. Tome trozos pequeños.

122. Tome sorbos pequeños.

123. Baje su barbilla.

124. ¿Le duele?

125. ¿Tiene dificultad al pasar o tragar?

126. Are you hungry?	126. ¿Tiene hambre?
127. Are you thirsty?	127. ¿Tiene sed?
128. Do you want to eat?	128. ¿Quiere usted comer?
129. Do you want more?	129. ¿Quiere usted más?
130. Do you like it?	130. ¿Le gusta?
131. Did you eat breakfast?	131. ¿Usted desayunó?
132. What did you eat?	132. ¿Que comió usted?

Orientation:
La orientación:

133. What day is it?	133. ¿Qué día es?
134. What month is it?	134. ¿Qué mes es?
135. What year?	135. ¿Qué año?
136. What is your name?	136. ¿Cuál es su nombre?
137. Where are you?	137. ¿Dónde estás?
138. Why are you here?	138. ¿Por qué está aquí?
139. Are you married?	139. ¿Esta casado? (to a man)
	OR ¿Esta casada? (to a woman)
140. Do you have a husband?	140. ¿Tiene usted un esposo?
141. Do you have a wife?	141. ¿Tiene usted una esposa?
142. What is your wife's name?	142. ¿Cuál es el nombre de su esposa?
143. What is your husband's name?	143. ¿Cuál es el nombre de su esposo?
144. Do you have children?	144. ¿Tiene usted hijos?
145. What are their names?	145. ¿Cuáles son sus nombres?
146. Where do you live?	146. ¿Donde usted vive?

147. What is the season?

147. ¿Cuál es la estación?

148. Spring.

148. Primavera.

149. Summer.

149. Verano.

150. Autumn.

150. Otoño

151. Winter.

151. Invierno.

152. Is it daytime?

152. ¿Es de día?

153. Is it nighttime?

153. ¿Es de noche?

154. What time is it?

154. ¿Qué hora es?

Perception:
La percepción:

155. Blue

155. Azul

156. Red

156. Rojo

157. Yellow

157. Amarillo

158. Orange

158. Naranja

159. Green

159. Verde

160. Purple

160. Morado

161. Black

161. Negro

162. White

162. Blanco

163. Brown

163. Café.

164. Square

164. Cuadrado

165. Triangle

165. Triángulo

166. Circle

166. El círculo

167. Cube

167. El cubo

168. Draw me a picture of yourself.

168. Haga un dibujo de usted mismo.

169. Draw me a clock.

169. Dibújeme un reloj.

170. Draw me a house.

170. Dibújeme una casa.

171. Draw me a flower.

171. Dibújeme una flor.

172. Please write your name.

172. Por favor escriba su nombre.

Swallow Precautions:
Precauciones al tragar:

173. You must sit up for thirty minutes.
173. Usted debe sentarse por treinta minutos.

174. You can only drink thickened liquids.
174. Usted puede beber líquidos espesos.

175. Please swallow twice.

175. Trague dos veces.

176. Please tuck your chin down.

176. Por favor baje su barbilla.

Encouragement:
El estímulo:

177. Terrific!

177. Magnífico!

178. Excellent.

178. Excelente.

179. Very Good.

179. Muy Bueno.

180. Good.

180. Bueno.

181. Keep Trying.

181. Siga Intentando lo.

182. Please stop.

182. Por favor pare.

183. Hurry up, please.

183. Dése prisa, por favor.

184. We don't want to be late.

184. Nosotros no queremos llegar tarde.

185. I cannot.

185. (Yo) no puedo.

186. Yes, you can.

186. Sí, (usted) puedes.

187. I will show you.

187. Yo le mostraré.

188. Are you sure?

189. That may be difficult but I will try.

190. Will there be anything else?

191. I would be glad to.

192. Everything is fine now.

193. What is the matter?

194. Yes, I know.

195. Yes, I could do that.

196. I will take that.

197. Wonderful.(perfect)

198. I believe so.

199. Of course (why not)

188. ¿Está usted seguro?

189. Eso puede ser difícil pero yo lo trataré

190. ¿Habrá algo más?

191. Yo me alegraría de.

192. Todo está ahora bien.

193. Cuál es la problema?

194. Sí, yo sé.

195. Sí, yo podría hacer eso.

196. Yo tomaré eso.

197. Maravilloso (perfecto)

198. Yo creo que sí.

199. Claro. (Por supuesto)

Created by Jacqueline Thrash, OTR, with assistance of Maya Hingorany, MS CCC SLP and Reshmi Saraladevi, MS CCC SLP

Translated using Transparent Language Presentation Program, Languages of the World, v4.01 2002.

Additional translations by Vidal Bugarin (Mexico).

Accuracy verification by Profesor de español, César Vallejo, Pasadena City College, CA.

Notes:

Notes:

Notes:

THEORY

As an occupational, physical, or speech therapist, you'll work with people from all over the world, for example:

• An (American) English speaking OT has a client from China, Mexico, Senegal, or Guadaloupe, and doesn't speak Mandarin, Spanish, Wolof, or French. She took Latin in high school.

• A Mexican American OT is working in an Adult Day setting with primarily Armenian clients. The clients have Limited English Proficiency (LEP), and the therapist doesn't speak Armenian.

• An SLP trained in India has a client from Brazil, but the speech therapist doesn't speak Brazilian Portuguese.

• A Philippine trained PT has relocated to the USA, and while awaiting PT certification, is working as a rehab aide along side of an OTR. The client is from Ethiopia, and neither of them speaks Amharic. The Aide's English is in the beginning stages, and the client doesn't speak English.

These are only a few of the scenarios possible. The World Federation of Occupational Therapy (WFOT) has 51 member countries, and, therefore, the possibility of a language barrier, both for clients or therapists, is exponential.

These chapters on Theory, Broadening Your Horizons, and Learning Social Greetings in Multiple Languages will help you understand why you need to use the phrases at the beginning of this book. They will also help you interface with people from all over the world, even if briefly.

Background:

In 1985, the Office of Minority Health (OMH) was established by the U.S. Department of Health and Human Services (HHS). It advises the Secretary and the Office of Public Health and Science on public health program activities affecting American Indians and Alaska Natives, Asian Americans, Blacks/African Americans, Hispanics/Latinos, Native Hawaiians, and other Pacific Islanders.

It was established "to improve and protect the health of racial and ethnic minority populations through the development of health policies and programs that will eliminate health disparities". http://www.omhrc.gov/OMH/sidebar/aboutOMH.htm

Prior to this executive order of 1985, the Older Americans Act was signed into law on July 14 1965. It established the Administration on Aging within the Department of Health, Education and Welfare, and called for the creation of State Units on Aging. http://www.aoa.dhhs.gov/prof/adddiv/adddiv.asp

However, in reviewing history, and its contribution (born out of struggle and sacrifice), we must look first at The Civil Rights Act of 1964.

Title VI of the Civil Rights Act of 1964 provides, "no person in the United States shall, on the ground of race, color, or national origin, be excluded from participation in, denied the benefits of, or be subjected to discrimination under any program or activity receiving federal financial assistance." 42 U.S.C. 2000d.

History:

Acknowledgement must be given to the African American community as a whole, and specifically to the leaders of the Civil Rights Movement, which has made it possible for **all** Americans to enjoy the freedom promised by the Civil Rights Act of 1964. Other groups, such as women, gays, and Americans with Disabilities have benefited from the efforts, sacrifices (even to the point of loss of life, i.e. Medgar Evers, Dr. Martin Luther King Jr, and Malcolm X, among others) and the legislation that came about as a result of the Civil Right Movement.

But, before appreciating the results of the Civil Rights Act, we must first investigate and understand *why* we would need it in the first place.

Historically, (North) American society has been hierarchical. According to Michael Carter, PhD, Cultural Anthropologist, it is based on the socially constructed concepts of "class", "race" and "gender" (Carter, 2006). In order to understand this, we must look at the *history* of the field of cultural anthropology.

In studying cultural anthropology, we learned that Henry Lewis Morgan, father of Anthropology, believed that all societies are based on unilateral evolution; which is hierarchical in nature. This hierarchy was divided into savagery, barbaric, and civilized. Most of us have heard (and possibly used) these terms, but may not know the origins. This body of thought ruled from approximately 1859 to the 1940s. (Carter, 2006).

Morgan believed that all societies go through this evolution, and the most evolved are "civilized". "These 19th-century unilineal evolution theories claimed that societies start out in a *primitive* state and gradually become more *civilized* over time, and equated Western civilization of technology and culture with progress. He proposed a unilineal scheme of evolution from primitive to modern, through which he believed societies progressed. His evolutionary views of the three major stages of social evolution, savagery, barbarism, and civilization, were proposed in *Ancient Society*. They are divided by technological inventions, like fire, bow, pottery in <u>savage</u> era, domestication of animals, agriculture, metalworking in <u>barbarian</u> era and alphabet and writing in <u>civilization</u> era. (Wikipedia). This, being an ethnocentric belief, was used as the basis for the concept of "race", which was the basis and justification of slavery in the Americas.

According to the lectures of Carter, class is defined as "the differential distribution of a form of value, i.e. money, knowledge, social contacts (network)". He explained that "class", "race", "whiteness", and "gender" are socially constructed, and not biological. He illuminated that American society is divided into classes, and the factors of class division can be opportunity, education, status, privilege, "gender", and "race" (Carter, 2006).

Prior to taking cultural anthropology, in my study of the contrast and nexus of African American and European American cultures, I, intuitively, noticed that American society's socially constructed division put European Americans (whites) on the top, and African Americans (previously referred to as black, Negroes, and 'colored') on the bottom. Asian Americans and Hispanic/Latin Americans fell somewhere in between. Audrey Smedley, professor of anthropology at Virginia Commonwealth University, describes this in Race in 21st Century America: Social Origins of the Idea of Race, "Human varieties formed a natural hierarchy, with Europeans on top and Africans on the bottom, and with all other 'races' located in between" (Smedley, p 16).

The division of society didn't start out by color; it was based on property ownership. Those with property had rights; those without did not. According to Carter, Karl Marx divided class by owners of a mode of production (factory owners) and workers of the mode of production (labor force). Those with money could invest in property and business, thus controlling the labor force (Carter, 2006).

In studying "the Peculiar Institution" of slavery with Dr. Ray Richardson, in African American history (Africa to America before 1865), we learned that slavery was the labor force prominent in the development and prosperity of United States of America. Even those who didn't "own" slaves prospered through the industrialization of the products of slavery: cotton, textiles, tobacco, etc. Later, what was initially a property-based hierarchy (class system) became a color-based hierarchy (Richardson, 1994).

It was even written into the constitution in article I section 2 with the "3/5s rule", and later reinforced with the prevalence of the "one drop rule" which "holds that a person with even a tiny portion of non-white ancestry ("one drop of non-white blood") should be classified as "colored"" (Wikipedia.com). This belief system was reinforced by Morgan's tripartite hierarchy of civilized, barbaric, and savagery. It was easy to continue to believe and justify the lie that people of color are less than "white" people, when society called people of color barbaric and savage. This lie became hegemonic or natural. It can still be seen today.

In studying African American history and culture (with both Richardson and Carter) and looking at the nexus of these areas of study with the results of the civil rights movement, we see that, when the group, which has been *perceived* as being at the bottom receives rights, freedom and dignity, then all those above also reap the benefits. Therefore, we owe a phenomenal debt to the African Americans as a group. They have been approximately ten percent of the population, however, they have made a huge impact for us all, not only in legislation, but also in also medicine, technology, literature, music, sports, as well as other areas. It is nearly impossible to dissect the contributions of African Americans from American culture. These threads of African American culture have become so integrated into the fabric of America, that we cannot see the "forest through the trees". It is not until we critically study and analyze the origins and contributions of people of color to the contemporary American culture that it becomes clear.

For further study in this area, please review the following movies: Eye on the Prize, Mississippi Burning, Malcolm X, Boycott, The Medgar Evers Story, Miss Evers Boys, Tuskegee Airmen, Soul Food, Down in the Delta, Something the Lord Made, Slavery & the Making of America (four disc set), Africans in America: America's Journey through Slavery (two disc set) and Bamboozled. Another excellent resource is Martin Scorsese Presents: The Blues: A Musical Journey (a seven disc series). There is also an abundance of literary works by and about African Americans available in the library and bookstores.

Legislation continues:

As a continuation of the legislation, which came from the Civil Rights Act; in 1990, the Americans with Disabilities Act extended protection from discrimination in employment and public accommodations to persons with disabilities.

Also, on August 11, 2000, President William Clinton, issued an executive order, #13166, to facilitate program guidelines and development for "Improving Access to Services for Persons with Limited English Proficiency".

It states,

> Minority elders may have a difficult time accessing federally funded
> Programs and services due to a lack of proficiency in the English language.
> To address this concern, President Clinton issued Order 13166, requiring
> that each federal agency prepares a plan by December 11, 2000, to improve
> access to its federally conducted programs and activities by limited English
> proficiency (LEP) persons. In response to the Executive Order, the Department
> of Justice (DOJ) and the Department of Health and Human Services, Office of
> Civil Rights (HHS/OCR) issued written policy guidelines. The guidelines define
> the legal responsibilities of providers who receive federal monies, and outline a
> range of flexible options available to agencies to comply with the law. To read
> Executive Order 13166, or guidelines issued by both DOJ and HHS/OCR, go to
> the address http://www.aoa.dhhs.gov/prof/civil_right/LEP/lep_whitehouse.asp

This long and hard journey led to the development of the concept of cultural competency.

What is Cultural Competency?

According to a guidebook published by the Administration on Aging, entitled <u>Achieving Cultural Competence: A Guidebook for Providers of Services to Older Americans and Their Families</u>, "Cultural competence is defined as a 'set of congruent behaviors, attitudes, and policies that come together in a system, agency, or among professionals and enables that system, agency, or those professionals to work effectively in cross–cultural situations."

They also state that "cultural competency is achieved by translating and integrating knowledge about individuals and groups of people into specific practices and policies applied in appropriate cultural settings. When professionals are culturally competent, they establish positive helping relationships, engage the client, and improve the quality of service they provide" (page 9). They further describe that the concept of cultural competency "has two primary dimensions: surface structure and deep structure. Borrowed from sociology and linguistics, these terms have been used to describe similar dimensions of culture and language" (page 9).

The Administration of Aging also lists the difficulties: "Racial and ethnic minorities face many barriers in receiving adequate care. These include difficulties with language and communication, feelings of isolation, encounters with service providers lacking knowledge of the client's culture and challenges related to the socio-economic status of the client" (page 9). They further describe methods for professional to obtain cultural competency, "This guidebook [Achieving Cultural Competence] argues that to achieve cultural competence, professionals must first have a sense of compassion and respect for people who are culturally different" (page 22).

Mikel Hogan, PhD, in her workbook, <u>The Four Skills of Cultural Diversity Competence</u>, defines cultural competency, or as she calls it, cultural diversity competence "as the ability to function with awareness, knowledge and interpersonal skill when engaging people of different background, assumptions, beliefs, values, and behaviors" (Hogan, p 3).

Hogan teaches college courses and private industry seminars regarding the process of becoming cultural diversity competent and uses an anthropological model of fieldwork principles to guide the process. In her Multilevel Training Model, she utilizes the anthropological defined term *cultural relativism,* which she defines as "the active processes of understanding oneself and others over one's life span while suspending judgment". She further describes the anthropological principles involved in this process as "self reflection and nonjudgement, emic contextualization and comparison, and the implementation of change through a holistic approach" (Hogan p 5). She defines the goal of cultural diversity competence as "the task is to gain understanding of human cultural diversity and to translate the cultural understanding into behaviors respectful of people, as well as to the organization policies that govern daily life" (Hogan p 6).

Why is Cultural Competency Important?

The website, http://www.diversityrx.org/HTML/MOCPT1.htm
includes an excellent article, entitled <u>Cultural Competence Practice and Training: Overview Why is Cultural Competence Important for Health Professionals?</u> They describe that "lack of awareness about cultural differences can make it difficult for both providers and patients to achieve the best, most appropriate care. Despite all our

similarities, fundamental differences among people arise from nationality, ethnicity, and culture, as well as from family background and individual experiences. These differences affect health beliefs, practices, and behavior on the part of both patient and provider, and also influence the expectations that patient and provider have of each other" (diversityrx).

In researching this topic for this book, I learned that becoming culturally competent is a development process, which includes not only empathy, genuine care and concern, but also an internal exploration of our own prejudices, beliefs, and biases, and modifying these beliefs to include other cultures. It also includes learning about cultural differences and practices, to provide more effective health care. I had already started this process in the late 1960s because my grandmother's grandfather from Virginia had slaves. When I was nine years old, my grandmother took me to his house in Mathews, Virginia, and told me stories. I knew at that age that it was wrong, and I wanted to change my attitudes so they would be different than my grandmother's. I spent the next 30 years on the process, and am glad I have. I have learned so much about myself and other people, and enjoyed the resultant open mind and heart that comes from learning about other cultures and peoples.

Hogan discusses that culture is both subjective and objective, as well as multilevel and dynamic. In her workbook, she describes "the twelve aspects of culture or ethnicity to include History, Social Status Factors, Social Group Interaction Patters: Intragroup and Intergroup, Value Orientations, Language and Communication: Verbal and Nonverbal, Family Life Processes, Healing Beliefs and Practices, Religion, Art and Expressive Forms, Diet/Foods, Recreation, and Clothing" (Hogan p 18). Through the use of her workbook, a person can grow from being ethnocentric to a state of diversity competence.

She mentions that culture is dynamic and multilevel. She does state that even Anglo Europeans have a culture, even though it may not be obvious to members of that group. Many Anglo Americans think that their "culture" is the norm, and therefore it seems invisible or bland (vanilla). In comparison to other cultures, it may look like us Anglos don't have a culture, however, Hogan illuminates the "Aspects of U.S. Mainstream/National Culture" in the Appendix, and as a member of that group, I would have to say she describes the "Anglo" culture accurately.

By learning about our own culture, as well as the culture of others around us, we can begin to understand the complexity, and dynamics of culture of humankind. This will facilitate communication and cooperation between the groups. It starts, however, with looking inward, self-reflection.

For example, do we think we are prejudiced? Do we think that every one is like us, and our values work for others, or should work for others? (Called *ethnocentric* by the cultural anthropologists). Are we able to put our attitudes and beliefs about how things "should" be aside in order to include their culture, and thus see and treat the client effectively? (The practice of *cultural relativism*). Do our prejudices overflow onto the other staff members from other countries or ethnicities?

For example, we all have encountered attitudes of prejudice; from people in general, other staff, as well as clients. It is human nature to want to believe that we are great, or as Eddie Thrash, music producer and educator, puts it "be the best you can be". In the western society, through competition, many try to be the "best (not of ourselves, but of the group); and this often results in looking at others as inferior, or not as good. This creates separatism, which is the seed of racism, sexism, etc. We see this in even the littlest matters, such as comparing clothing, incomes, cars, or looks. When I was working at my first OT job, in 1988, some of the other OTs were concerned with who had the latest shoes, slacks, or styles in general. I had just come out of OT school, and was establishing myself in my career (and paying student loans) so my funds were limited, and I didn't have the "latest" fashions. This is one minor incidence of separatism.

How about if the client is obviously racist or prejudiced against the staff or the other clients of other ethnicities? This goes against what many therapists believe. Therefore, it results in conflict. Don't I still have a responsibility to provide the best possible service (therapy) to this individual, despite our differences in beliefs and attitudes? Yes. I have had clients who were bigoted, and had to work through our difference of beliefs in order to provide thorough service.

I have chosen to only briefly cover this broad topic, cultural competency, as this book (set) Common Phrase Translation (OT/PT/ST) is only one method of addressing cultural competency, through language. Hogan describes language and communication as one of the 12 aspects of culture, and elaborates that this aspect of culture is subdivided into verbal communalization (or language) and nonverbal communication (Hogan p 19-20).

To see further discussion on language refer to Chapter 2, Broadening Your Horizons. For further education regarding cultural competency and the internal exploration of attitudes and beliefs there are several seminars, college courses and books available. For additional resources on cultural competence, please see Review of Literature, for further study and Appendix B: Cultural Competency Resources.

As mentioned in the preface, the idea of this book, Common Phrase Translation: Spanish for English Speakers For Occupational Therapy, Physical Therapy and Speech Therapy was born out of necessity. I noticed the necessity when I was working with clients with Limited English Proficiency (LEP) both in Arizona as well as Northern and Southern California.

In Arizona, during my first occupational therapy job in 1988, we had a Mexican client who had a stroke and had difficulty sitting upright. When she sat in the hall, she often lost her sitting balance, and leaned over the wheelchair armrest. It looked uncomfortable. We (the staff) would help her reposition to midline. One day she said something to me in Spanish, and I asked Rachel Cano, LVN (Mexican American) what she said. She translated, "Don't push on me like a sack of potatoes". Rachel taught me my first full sentence (other than social niceties), "Don't look like a sack of potatoes" in Spanish. So, all I had to do was say this (No se mira combien un saco de papas), and the client would sit up straight. It worked.

Another later example, in a skilled nursing facility (SNF) in Southern California, where the nursing and therapy staff were primarily Spanish, Tagalog and English speaking, we had a Russia born client who spoke very little English. We did have one Russian born and trained PT, Marina, however, when she wasn't in the facility, the client appeared sad, withdrawn, and isolated. None of the other staff (myself included) spoke Russian. I had to use gestures to communicate, and found this inadequate. What if there was a book with common OT phrases in Russian? One that I could prop open and read!

The full version book, <u>Common Phrase Translation: Occupational Therapy</u> (and PT/ST) is being written as one method of addressing the problem of language and communication, during evaluation and treatment by translating common phrases used by therapists into over 40 languages. This resource will allow the therapist to improve the possibilities of communicating effectively with the client, in their language, thus improving the effectiveness and outcome of the therapeutic process/rehabilitation. The use of the client's native language provides respect for their culture and language, instead of expecting them to assimilate and learn "English". As previously stated, I have divided the 40 languages into individual language books (you are reading one!).

In the near future, I will be adding an audio CD of the phrases in the workbook to assist the therapist with proper pronunciation. Until then, you can hear pronunciation of some common phrases (travel and conversation related) on Transparent Language Presentation Program, 1997-2002, Languages of the World v4.01, which includes 101 languages. The pilot of this audio project is in process under the supervision of Jeff Rudisill, Instructor in the Performing Arts and Broadcasting Program and Teresa Baxter, General Manager of Lancer Radio, both from Pasadena City College.

In order to understand the nexus of culture and medicine, we must briefly look at medical anthropology, which is relevant to the study of cultural competence and allied health (therapies).

Medical Anthropology & Allied Health (OT/PT/ST)

The "health affects" mentioned in the previous section on cultural competency are studied in the field of medical anthropology both from a biological and a cultural aspect. Cultural practices and behaviors can have a biological affect, often referred to as sociobiology (Carter, 2006).

According to the Society of Medical Anthropologists, a subgroup of the American Anthropological Association, "Medical Anthropology is a sub field of anthropology that draws upon social, cultural, biological, and linguistic anthropology to better understand those factors which influence health and well being (broadly defined), the experience and distribution of illness, the prevention and treatment of sickness, healing processes, the social relations of therapy management, and the cultural importance and utilization of pluralistic medical systems." http://www.medanthro.net/index.html

In the following example, this can be illustrated by the historical and cultural practice of African Americans eating certain foods, and later developing high blood pressure, diabetes, and heart disease. In order to fully understand this relationship, we must, again, look critically at the history of the United States of America and it's effects.

For example, during (and after) slavery, the African American woman working in the plantation house kitchen would save the scraps from the "Masters" table, and take them to her family to supplement the foods from her family's garden. Meat was hard to come by for the enslaved Africans and African Americans, and they made use of the innards and scraps that were to be thrown away (intestines, gizzards, liver, kidneys, and pig feet) as protein supplement. They would improve the flavor with salt, and spices, and by frying it in lard (pig fat). They also added refined sugar to foods to improve the flavor. This food source, often referred to as "soul food", was therefore, high in salt, fat and sugar. The continuation of the culture of "soul food" has led to many African Americans having medical problems that stemmed from diet.

Eddie Thrash, African American, described his enlightenment in the early 1980s when he realized if he ate the way his ancestors ate, then he would die of the same diseases they did (his mother died of high blood pressure-aneurysm at age 33; and his aunt (who raised him) died of diabetes and stroke). He compared and contrasted the foods of West Africa and those mass-produced in the United States of America through industrial agriculture. He realized that African Americans were eating many foods that were not typical of their environment and culture from Africa (in Africa: yams, cassava melons, couscous, millet, rice, fruits and vegetables, chicken, fish, as well as others) and were eating refined flour, sugar, white potatoes, and pork. He changed his diet in order to save his life. (Eddie Thrash, 2005).

Professor Tom Hogue, of Glendale Community College described the use of language to improve medical services as a cultural component of medical anthropology. Medical anthropology intersects with allied health profession services (OT/PT/ST) through the concept of improving medical care treatment through the use of the client's native language, and incorporating the cultural practices in provision of services. This area of study (the development of this book) actually intersects four areas, allied health, cultural and medical anthropology, and linguistics. A viable example of these nexuses: the therapist can improve functional outcome of therapy services by being sensitive to and aware of the cultural differences and how it effects communication, as well as learning at least a bit of the client's language.

As previously mentioned in the foreword, Dr. Guy McCormack, OTR, explains that language can be a bridge or a barrier. This barrier can be interpersonal as well as clinical. Wanting to be successful in assisting the client in reaching their rehabilitation goals is a large component of the role of the therapist; and can be seen in the nexus between these four areas. By using the native language, the (English speaking) therapist increases the possibility of effective communication, and also builds and maintains rapport between the therapist and non-English speaking client. This improved communication leads to an increase in positive outcome in the accomplishment of therapy goals. The areas of concern in improving communication practices and thus the therapeutic outcome, are metalinguistics, roles between men and women, as well as what a person may and may not do relating to their culture. For further elaboration, see <u>Multicultural Manners</u> in the Review of Literature.

Cultural Interfacing:

When interfacing two or more cultures, problems may arise from the differences in cultural practices and beliefs which can lead to misunderstanding and conflict. Initially, when I began writing this book, I was reluctant to list generalizations about one culture or another. I recognized that an individual within a culture has their own personal preferences which may or may not coincide with the culture at large. Therefore, if we say "all women or all men in such and such culture believe, do, or practice such and such" we would be incorrect. I, especially, didn't want to indicate that "*all* people from a culture do such and such a thing". There are always exceptions.

For example, a previous boyfriend, Manuel, who is African American, Native American and Russian Jew said to me about 15 years ago, "Jackie, you're Scottish, why don't you play the bagpipes?" I replied, "Why don't you have a bone in your nose?" He laughed so hard that he almost fell off the couch. My point was that both of us are so far from our cultural roots, that we don't practice many of their cultural traditions.

Another example, I am of Germanic (German and Dutch) and British Island (English and Scottish) descent. Traditionally, some German people eat bratwurst with mustard and sauerkraut, and some British people eat Fish and Chips. I do like bratwurst, but I don't like mustard or sauerkraut. As far as fish goes, I only like mild fish, and maybe only three or four times a year. So, it would be a mistake to assume that because I am of German and British descent, that I like mustard, sauerkraut, or fish.

One more personal example, my husband, Eddie, who is African American, has adjusted his eating so he doesn't get the same diet and culture related illnesses that his ancestors got, by veering away from "Soul Food" which includes grits, chitterlings, ham hocks, fried chicken, chicken livers, and lard. Besides, he doesn't *like* chitterlings. He does like *some* traditionally African American foods, but to assume that he eats all of them would be a mistake.

Once, I heard a story about an African American man who on an airplane, and the passengers were being served dinner. In the row before this man, the flight attendant asked each passenger whether s/he wanted steak or chicken. When she got to this African American man, she just handed him the chicken dinner. He was offended. He thought she was stereotyping him by assuming that since he was African American, he ate (fried) chicken and watermelon.

As I said earlier, initially, I felt uncomfortable about making generalizations because there are so many variables and not every one follows all of the practices of their culture. From my culture, (Anglo-American, high school graduate from Virginia in 1977) for example, many (white) women are expected to grow up, get married, have 2-4 children, and become executive secretaries, if they work at all. Some (Anglo) women were encouraged to go to college, and often were encouraged to become involved in service occupations, such as administrative assistants, customer service, or nurses. When I was 20 and trying to decide what I wanted "to be when I grow up", I decided that I wanted to explore other parts of the United States, live in a multicultural neighborhood, and discover what my career would be based on what was inside of me, not what someone else said I should do. I used my own personal makeup and preferences as a guide; and didn't go for the "cultural expectations".

However, through my development as a culturally aware and culturally competent individual, I realize it is necessary to share some resources which I have been given, even though it is a "touchy" subject, this cultural interfacing.

I have found two resources for describing cultural practice differences of many cultures, <u>Caring for Patients from Different Cultures: Case Studies from American Hospitals</u>, by Geri-Ann Galanti, and <u>Multicultural Manners</u> by Norine Dresser. After the following introduction, I will include some examples of Hispanic, Mexican, and Latin American cultures from these books.

Galanti describes her book as "This book addresses the culture differences that create conflict and misunderstandings and that may result in inferior medical care".

Galanti warns about stereotyping, and indicates the difference between stereotyping and generalizing, "A stereotype and generalization may appear similar but they function very differently. An example is the assumption that Mexicans have large families. If I meet Rosa, a Mexican woman, and I say to myself, 'Rosa is Mexican; she must have a large family', I am stereotyping her. But if I think, Mexicans often have large families and wonder whether Rosa does, I am making a generalization" (Galanti, p 2). She adds "A stereotype is an ending point. No attempt is make to learn whether the individual in question fits the statement. A generalization, on the other hand is a beginning point. It indicates common trends, but further information is needed to ascertain whether the statement is appropriate to a particular individual" (Galanti, p 2).

Okay, here goes…..

Body Language and Physical Contact:

Norine Dresser, in her book, <u>Multicultural Manners</u>, discusses body language, and states that "when greeting, most Latinos expect body contact. Hugging and kissing on the cheek are acceptable for both the same and the opposite sex. The *abrazo* is commonplace— friends embrace and simultaneously pat each other on the back" (Dresser, p 13).
I, personally, know this to be true. A newspaper writer, Maria Pilar Jiminez from Columbia did an article about my accident and this book series in La Opiníon, a local Los Angeles Spanish newspaper. For the "interview" we corresponded in English and Spanish over the internet; it was easier for her to write in English than to speak it, and easier for

me to write in Spanish than to speak it. I never met her in person, but at the conclusion of our "interview", she sent me an *abrazo*.

Clasped Hands:

Ms. Dresser informs us "In Guatemala, when someone holds their hands together, it is a sign of death". They don't even want the babies to do it, because it is "especially ominous" (Dresser, p 17).

Gestures:

Dresser reminds us "gestures do not have universal meaning" (Dresser, p 19). A friendly gesture in one country or language system can be very offensive in another. I, in the past, have had to use body language and gestures to communicate with my limited English speaking clients. Unfortunately, it can be easy to make a mistake without knowing it.

Eye Contact:

Dresser explains a story about a newcomer from Mexico, Isabela, "who had been taught to avoid eye contact as a mark of respect to authority figures—teachers, employers, parents" (Dresser, a 22). I imagine doctors, nurses, and therapists would fall into this category. Dresser indicates that people from Latin America may also do this. This can cause misunderstandings with the dominant cultural practice of making direct eye contact during conversation. For the direct eye gazer, eye eversion can be thought of as dishonest, suspicious, sneaky, weak, or disrespectful. For the eye-averting individual, they might believe they are showing respect by averting their eyes.

One at a Time:

Dresser describes an experience of a man, Harold, who wanted to buy a TV, and the salesman was waiting on him, showing him TVs, and then the salesman suddenly disappeared and started helping another customer without finishing with the first man. Harold believed that once a salesperson starts with a particular customer, s/he should complete the task before assisting another customer. Eduardo, the salesman, was from Puerto Rico and the concept of one at a time didn't apply. "In Puerto Rico and other Latin American countries, a salesperson takes care of up to four people at a time. Not only that, a newcomer has priority over the previous customer" (Dresser, p 25-26). This situation can occur within the medical field service provision also.

Holidays:

Dresser lists an important Mexican holiday, Day of the Dead (Día de los Muertos). She describes, "On November 1st, All Saint's Day, families go to the cemetery, wash the tombstones, and decorate the graves of their loved ones with marigolds (zempazuchuitl). They believe that on November 2nd, All Soul's Day, the most recently deceased return to be with the living. In some parts of Mexico, people shoot off fireworks to guide the spirits' pathway home. Once returned, the family welcomes them by having their favorite foods placed on special altars called *ofrendas*" (Dresser, p 191). To read more, see her book, Multicultural Manners.

First Names:

"Americans tend to refer to each other by their first names. It is considered a sign of friendliness and equality. To use a first name for anyone other than a close friend, however, is both inappropriate and discourteous in most cultures, including European. Hospital personnel should refer to all adult patients as Mr., Miss, Ms., or Mrs., unless instructed otherwise" (Galanti, p 19-20).

Using Family to Translate-It Can Be Problematic:

Galanti informs us that many hospitals have difficulty maintaining sufficient interpreter staff to cover the diverse languages represented by the variety of immigrants to the United States. Often times, family members are used to interpret. However, within the Latin American culture, it is inappropriate for a male child (young or adult) to discuss the private parts of the mother, when it is necessary for her to have "female surgery". In one case, the son told his mother that a tumor would be removed from her abdomen area, when in fact, she was scheduled for a hysterectomy (Galanti, p 22).

Communication Style and Demeanor:

"A twenty-seven-year-old Mexican American named Alfredo Gomez was in traction with multiple fractures following a car accident. He whined continuously and incessantly summoned Helga, his German nurse, with the call light. Helga became very frustrated and angry with him and consequently adopted a stern and direct attitude. Alfredo's behavior changed only when his wife and sister arrived and gave him their full attention. They anticipated his every need, straightened his pillow and moistened his lips. Following their lead, Helga spoke more slowly and warmly to Alfredo, letting him know she understood what a frightening experience he had had. She also did what she could to make him more comfortable before he asked. As a result he quickly became less dependent and did not use the call light so frequently (Galanti, p 25).

I had an experience similar to this one. I was working with a Mexican American man of similar age, who had been in a car accident, and had open reduction internal fixation of the tibia and fibula with a "cage" on the outside of this lower leg. He was stuck in bed on traction, and had little company because his wife was at home with a small child. He didn't speak much English, and for stimulation, he enjoyed watching the Spanish TV station. One day, the TV station broke down, and he had little or no stimulation in Spanish. He looked so sad, that on the way home that night, I stopped at La Peña, a cultural center in Oakland, and bought him a novella written in Spanish. The next day I gave it to him. He gave me a big smile, and was visibly grateful.

For more examples, please read both books by Galanti and Dresser.

Review of Literature

In developing the idea of writing a book of common phrases translated into multiple languages, it was necessary to review the literature at hand. For my purposes, I was pleased that I didn't find this book already written; however, I did find a useful body of literature, which has helped in the development of my project.

1. Galanti, Geri-Ann. Caring for Patients from Different Cultures: Case Studies from American Hospitals. University of Pennsylvania Press, Philadelphia.

Caring for Patients from Different Cultures is a 171 page, 6 x 9 inch soft cover book which is divided into the following sections: Basic Concepts (including Anthropological concepts); Communication and Time Orientation; Pain; Religions, Beliefs and Customs; Dietary Practices; Family; Men and Women; Staff Relations; Birth; Death and Dying; Mental Health; Folk Medicine-Practices and Perspectives and of course, Conclusion.

Galanti uses case studies from American hospitals, gleaned from experiences of numerous nurses and other health care professionals, as well as her own professional experiences. She has used these case studies to teach Cultural Competency Training on the university and private workshop level. Her book is an excellent work, which combines both anthropology as well as health practices and interactions. The reader has a better understanding of not only what occurs, but why. It is a good resource for therapists, nurses, and other health care professionals.

2. Dresser, Norine. Multicultural Manners: New Rules of Etiquette for a Changing Society. John Wiley & Sons., Inc. New York.

Multicultural Manners, is a 285 page, 6 x 9 inch soft cover book which is divided into the following sections: The New Rules of Communication, (Body Language, Child Rearing Practices, Classroom Behavior, Clothing, Colors, Foodways, Gifts, Luck and Supernatural Forces, Male/Female Relations, Miscellany, Prejudice, Time, and Verbal Expressions); Rules for Holidays and Worship (New Year's Celebrations, On Other Ethnic Holidays, and At Places of Worship); Multicultural Health Practices: Remedies and Rituals (Asian Pacific, Caribbean, European, Latin American, Muslim).

Dresser is a folklorist- "someone who studies customs, rituals and beliefs". From this perspective, she gives a different view of people and culture than Galanti. Dresser uses the sections to compare and contrast several cultures simultaneously; thus giving a multi-faceted picture for the reader. The section on Body Language would be especially helpful to augment Common Occupational Therapy Phrase Translation Workbook (aw well as PT & ST). This book is also an excellent resource for the therapist, and other health professionals who are interested in learning more about other cultural customs, beliefs, and practices.

3. Hogan, Mikel. <u>The Four Skills of Cultural Diversity Competence A Process for Understanding and Practice</u>. Third Edition. Thompson Brooks/Cole.

<u>The Four Skills of Cultural Diversity Competence A Process for Understanding and Practice</u> is a 150 page, 8 ½ x 11-inch soft cover workbook. It discusses the anthropological theory of humans and culture, the stages involved in sociocultural awareness and the process of becoming cultural diversity competent. It includes practical tasks and small group situations for gaining these skills, as well as the implications for society in the event that these diverse groups learn to understand one another and communicate and work together effectively. It is an excellent resource for learning about culture, and the problems when cultures clash, as well as a practical tool for self-development.

4. Chase, Robert; Medina de Chase, Clarisa B. <u>An Introduction to Spanish for Health Care Workers: Communication and Culture</u>. Yale Language Series, Yale University Press. New Haven & London.

<u>An Introduction to Spanish for Health Care Workers</u> is a 358 page, 7 x 10 inch soft cover book with accompanying CD. It is divided into sections, Hello, I am the Doctor; How Are You; What is the Matter; The Receptionist; The Family; The Pharmacy; Diet and Nutrition; The Physical Exam; The Past (Preterit) Tense; Taking Medical History; Hospitalizations, Dentistry, and Mental Health; and Maternity and Safer Sex.

Chase and Medina de Chase have presented a thorough language and culture study book (text book with CD) for those interested in learning Spanish, or those who would be working with Spanish speaking clientele. It is primarily for health care workers such as doctors, dentists, pharmacists, nurses, etc. It does list translation professional titles: "physical therapist", "respiratory therapist", and "speech therapist". It does not include "occupational therapist". Unfortunately it does not include phrases for OT, PT, or ST in the translation and practice sections. It can, however, be very useful for the therapist who is interested in improving their conversational and health care related Spanish, because it provides written self-tests, and an audio CD. This would be a good resource, also.

5. <u>Speedy Spanish for Physical Therapists</u>. Baja Books, Santa Barbara CA.

<u>Speedy Spanish for Physical Therapists</u> is a 12 page, 3 ¼ x 5 ½ inch pocket book which includes the following sections: Numbers, Greetings, Basic Anatomical Terms, Patient Complaints, Basic Examination, Modalities/Treatment, Exercises, Orthopedic Surgeries, Wheelchair/Walker/Crutches, and Occupational Therapy.

Baja Books has put together a very nice pocket size reference for the PT (and a few phrases for the OT) to use on a daily basis, when speaking with Spanish therapy clients. It includes both the correct spelling (in Spanish) as well as the phonetic conversions.

6. Speedy Spanish for Medical Personnel. Baja Books, Santa Barbara CA.

Speedy Spanish for Medical Personnel is a 12 page, 3 ¼ x 5 ½ inch pocket book which includes the following sections: Numbers, Greetings, Basic Anatomical Terms, Patient Complaints, Basic Examination, Abdominal Disorders, Allergies/Breathing Problems, Burns/Chest Pain, Diabetes/Neurological Disorders, OB/GYN, Overdose/Poisoning, and Seizures/Trauma. It is primarily for intake (nursing or medical) examination or evaluation. It can be useful for the therapist for general health related phrases.

7. Speedy Spanish for Public Health Personnel. Baja Books, Santa Barbara CA.

Speedy Spanish for Public Health Personnel is a 12 page, 3 ¼ x 5 ½ inch pocket book which includes the following sections: Basic Phrases, Small Talk/Appointments, Patient Info/Taking Vitals; Numbers/Days & Months, Sexually Transmitted Diseases, HIV Screening/Birth Control, Immunizations, TB Screening & Chest X Ray/Mammogram, Problem Drinking/Depression & Anxiety, Medical Assessment, Injections & Meds. It is primarily for public health clinics and medical offices.

8. Iwata, Carla M. & Harvey, Charlene D. Language Translations: Functional Terms in Occupational Therapy. (Spanish). AOTA Press. Bethesda MD. (out of print).

Language Translations: Functional Terms in Occupational Therapy (Spanish) was a master's project for Carla M. Iwata (OT) and Charlene D. Harvey (OT) for Samuel Merritt College in Oakland CA. It is 8 ½ x 11, soft cover and spiral bound. At the time of this writing, it was out of print. From reviewing the front matter, it seemed to be a very useful and specific OT book for use with Spanish speaking clients. It is unfortunate that it isn't available for the general OT practitioner and OT students. I would have liked to have it years ago when I started working with Spanish speaking OT clients.

9. Curtis, Kathleen A. & Newman, Peggy DeCelle. The PTA Handbook: Keys to Success in School and Career for the Physical Therapy Assistant. Slack Inc.

The PTA Handbook is a 306 page, 8 ½ x 11 soft cover book. Chapter 18 entitled Diversity and Cultural Competence in Physical Therapy discusses issues of diversity in the physical therapy profession, the diversity of the clients of physical therapy, culture and its implications on physical therapy service provision, developing cultural competence, and includes a one page exercise of self evaluation.

10. Joyce, Esperanza Villanueva, & Villanueva, Maria Elena. Say it in Spanish: A Guide for Health Care Professionals (1996). W.B. Saunders Company

Say it in Spanish is a 335 page, 6 x 9 inch soft cover book. It is primarily for nursing and emergency personnel. It has 32 chapters which include: emergency room; home visits; dental visits; hospital; secretaries (unit clerical staff); admitting; in the patient's room; X-Ray department; laboratory; pharmacy; meals; discharge planning; physical exam greetings and common expressions; commands; phrases; cognates; numbers; time; colors, seasons, months, days, cardinal points; members of the family; alphabet; accents; gender of nouns; adjectives and pronouns; simple questions; exclamations; negatives & affirmatives; verbs; a cultural perspective; and home cures and popular beliefs.

It is a useful resource clinical reference and textbook for health care students.

11. Kelz, Rochelle K. <u>Conversational Spanish for Medical Personnel</u>. (1982) John Wiley & Sons.

<u>Conversational Spanish</u> is a 538 page, 6 x 9 inch, soft cover book, covering "essential expressions, questions, and directions for medical personnel to facilitate conversation with Spanish-speaking patients and coworkers". It includes 9 chapters with topics: Pronunciation, Essential Grammar, Common Expressions, Numerical Expressions, Anatomic and Physiological Vocabulary, Conversation for Medical and Paramedical personnel, Conversations for administrative personnel, authorizations and signatures, crucial vocabulary for medical personnel, and two appendices: English-Spanish vocabulary, and Spanish-English vocabulary.

It also, is primarily for nursing (and emergency personnel). It is a useful resource for health care students, and it includes anatomical diagrams.

References:

Carter, Michael J. PhD, Professor of Anthropology, Glendale Community College, CA.

Cross T., Bazron, B., Dennis, K., & Isaacs, M. (1989). <u>Towards a culturally competent system of care</u>, volume I. Washington, D.C.: Georgetown University Child Development Center, CASSP Technical Assistance Center.

Dresser, Norine. <u>Multicultural Manners: New Rules of Etiquette for a Changing Society</u>. John Wiley & Sons., Inc. New York.

Galanti, Geri-Ann. <u>Caring for Patients from Different Cultures: Case Studies from American Hospitals</u>. University of Pennsylvania Press, Philadelphia.

Hogan, Mikel. <u>The Four Skills of Cultural Diversity Competence A Process for Understanding and Practice</u>. Third Edition. Thompson Brooks/Cole.

Hogan, Mikel, PhD, Professor Anthropology, California State University, Fullerton.

Hogue, Tom. MS Anthropology. Glendale Community College, CA

Richardson, Ray, PhD, Department Chair of African American Studies, at Laney College, Oakland CA.

Smeldley, Audrey. Race in 21st Century America: Social Origins of the Idea of Race, (2000) Michigan.

Thrash, Eddie J., Independent Record Producer, Educator, and African American. Interviews 1995-2005. http://www.pinkiemae.com

http://cecp.air.org/cultural/Q_important.htm

http://www.diversityrx.org/HTML/MOCPT1.htm

http://www.aoa.dhhs.gov/prof/addiv/cultural/addiv_cult.asp

http://www.amsa.org/programs/gpit/cultural.cfm

http://www.medanthro.net/definition.html

BROADENING YOUR HORIZONS

Language and Culture:

Through the study of anthropology, specifically the areas of language and culture, it is understood that language is an integral part of every culture, and that each group has a language, whether oral, gestured, or written. We also know that language from one culture can influence another culture, e.g. beatnik, cool jazz, and hip hop expressions which started with the African American culture, were adopted by other groups such as European Americans, Asian Americans, and Latin or Hispanic Americans. It is also known that as peoples migrate from place to place, a country can have more than one language spoken.

Linguistics and Linguistic Anthropology:

Linguistics is the study of the human language. Nancy Bonvillain describes language as "an integral part of human behavior. It is the primary means of interaction between people. Speakers use language to convey their thoughts, feelings, intentions, and desires to others. Language is enriched by the uses that people make of it. These uses, and the meanings transmitted, are situational, social, and cultural". She describes cultural meanings as being expressed both "in a symbolic sense of words and by the ways that interlocutors evaluate communicative behavior" (Bonavillian, p 1). She also describes language as a "communicative system consisting of formal units that are integrated through processes of combination. This includes "components of sound, structure and meanings (Bonvillain, p 7).

Linguistic Anthropology is the study of humans (anthropology) through the languages they use (Wikipedia). Wendy Fonarow, PhD, Linguistic Anthropologist, describes the components of phonology, morphology, and semantics. These words may be unfamiliar to the layperson and can be described as follows: phonology (accent); lexicon (regional vocabulary); and syntax (grammatical rules and sentence word order) (Thrash, 2005). Fonarow further indicates that languages have a formal and informal component. She describes code switching as using formal with one's parents, and informal with one's peers; and knowing when to switch. (Fonarow, 2005).

Mikel Hogan describes the use of both verbal and nonverbal components of language and communication. She indicates that these components can vary from culture to culture, and can give rise to much misunderstanding (Hogan, p 20).

In occupational therapy, physical therapy, and speech therapy (often referred to as the allied health professions), language is used by the client to express oneself, as well as bridge the gap between the client and therapist. The therapists' role is to assist the client in obtaining skills necessary to make functional gains and reach functional goals related to improving their abilities related to every day living. (Huh? For a breakdown of areas covered by *each* of these therapies, see front matter just past the "other books available by Jacqueline Thrash:" for the OT, PT, and ST categories).

The therapist needs to use language to communicate instructions, feedback, precautions, encouragement and praise. It makes sense for these therapists to be able to communicate, even simply, with the client in his or her own language. It is an appropriate treatment concern because these allied health professions look at the whole person: psychological, social, physical, emotional and intellectual. The therapist's knowledge of (and willingness to use it) the client's language can help improve the self-esteem of the client, and therefore, positively affect their health and progress. The client can be understandable fearful because of the medical problems which necessitate therapy services, and may very well feel ashamed and isolated. The use of the client's language demonstrates that the therapist cares enough to learn about the client's culture, and therefore, by association, probably cares for the client. It is best to use the formal version of a language when speaking with clients, until they indicate that you can use the informal. I have tried to put the more formal, thus respectful, version of the languages in this book. Better to err on the side of caution.

Language and Countries:

When looking at language translating software, in preparation for this book, I noticed many with the more common European languages, and few with the languages of the original peoples. In this book set <u>Common Phrase Translation</u> (OT, PT, ST), I have (at least) included <u>some</u> of the languages of original peoples. I have, by necessity, also included the more widely used European languages. I, did, however, choose to include languages *outside* of Europe, in order to keep from making this just another "euro centric" book; thus, keeping with the purpose of cultural competence.

As a result of the Age of Exploration, 1414 to 1506, several of the European countries sent exploration expeditions to other countries and continents in search (and procurement) of resources, whether land, agriculture, artifacts, gold, indentured servants and/or slaves. This colonization (of Africa, the Pacific, the Americas) led to European languages such as English, Portuguese, Spanish, Dutch, and French becoming the national languages of these affected countries. Examples of the European language becoming the national language: English in what is now called United States, and Nigeria; Portuguese in Brazil and Angola; Spanish in Mexico, Columbia and Cuba; French in Guadeloupe and Senegal; and Russian in Armenia and Czech Republic. The Arabic language was also spread as well in the Middle East, and North Africa, with the spread of Islam

Below, I have included as a cross reference, of eleven languages and the countries which have them as a national language, such as:

Arabic: Algeria, Bahrain, Chad, Egypt, Eritrea, Iraq, Israel, Jordan, Kuwait, Lebanon, Libya, Mauritania, Morocco, Oman, Palestine, Qatar, Saudi Arabia, Somalia, Sudan, Syria, Tunisia, United Arab Emirates, and Yemen; **Castilian**: Northern Spain, Canary Islands, and Guinea; **Dutch**: Aruba, Belgium, Netherlands Antilles, and Netherlands, and Suriname; English: **English** (list includes both British English and American English) American Samoa, Anguilla, Antigua, Australia, Bahamas, Barbados, Barbuda, Belize,

Bermuda, Botswana, British Virgin Islands, Brunei, Cameroon, Canada, Cayman Islands, Cook Islands, Dominica, Ethiopia, Falkland Islands, Fiji, Gambia, Ghana, Gibraltar, Grenada, Guam, Guyana, India, Ireland, Israel, Jamaica, Kiribati, Kenya, Lesotho, Liberia, Malawi, Mauritius, Micronesia, Midway Island, Montserrat, Namibia, Nauru, New Zealand, Nigeria, Nike, Norfolk Island, Northern Mariana Islands, Pakistan, Palau, Papua New Guinea, Philippines, Pitcairn, Puerto Rico, Rwanda, St. Helena, St. Kitts-Nevis, St. Lucia, St.Vincent and the Grenadines, Seychelles, Sierra Leone, Singapore, Solomon Islands, Somalia, South Africa, Swaziland, Tokelau, Tonga, Trinidad and Tobago, Uganda, United Kingdom, US Virgin Islands, Vanuatu, Wake Islands, Western Samoa, Zambia, Zimbabwe. **French**: Andorra, Belgium, Benin, Burkina Faso, Burundi, Cameroon, Canada, Central African Republic, Chad, Comoros Islands, Congo, Cote d'Ivoire, Democratic Republic of Congo, Djibouti, French Guiana, French Polynesia, Gabon, Guadeloupe, Guinea, Haiti, Italy, Lebanon, Luxembourg, Madagascar, Mali, Martinique, Mayotte, Monaco, Morocco, New Caledonia, Niger, Reunion, Rwanda, Seychelles, Senegal, St. Pierre and Miguelon, Switzerland, Togo, United Kingdom, Vanuatu, Wallis and Futuna; **German**: Austria, Belgium, Denmark, Italy, Liechtenstein, Luxembourg, and Switzerland; **Italian**: San Marino, Slovenia, and Switzerland; **Kiswahili**: Democratic Republic of Congo, Kenya, Rwanda, and Tanzania. Mandarin: China, Singapore, Taiwan; **Portuguese**: Angola, Brazil, Cape Verde Islands, Guinea-Bissau, Mozambique, Sao Tome e Principe, and Timor Lorosae; **Russian**: Armenia, and Czech Republic; **Spanish**: Argentina, Bolivia, Chile, Columbia, Costa Rica, Cuba, Dominican Republic, Ecuador, El Salvador, Guatemala, Honduras, Mexico, Nicaragua, Panama, Paraguay, Peru, Puerto Rico, Uruguay, and Venezuela; **Welsh**: United Kingdom.

This will make it easier for the therapist who speaks one of these eleven languages. If you know one or more of these, you have a good chance of communicating with many peoples.

Of course, it is best if we take the time to learn at least a few phrases from the original language of these countries (such as Hindi in India, Wolof in Senegal, Kiswahili in Kenya and Tanzania), out of respect to the original peoples.

I recommend you practice at least the social greetings from the Learning Social Greetings in Multiple Languages chapter, and then if you need to, you can order the individual language book in another language.

In Appendix A, you can see a list of 228 countries, the number of "living" languages, and a cross reference to the languages translated in this book. For example, you are given a new client, from Senegal, and you have no idea what language they speak, so you quickly look in Appendix A. You note that they speak both Wolof (local language) and French. You are in luck; you speak a little French. So, you review the book on French for English Speakers, and grab a few social greetings from the Wolof section of Learning Social Greetings in Multiple Languages, out of respect. Voila! Or, another scenario, you don't know any French at all? Why not try the Wolof for English Speakers book if you are going to try a new language? Have fun!

References:

Bonvillain, Nancy. Language, Culture, and Communication: The Meaning of Messages.

Fonarow, Wendy, PhD, Linguistic Anthropologist, Glendale Community College, CA
    Lectures and notes on Culture and Communication 2005.

Thrash, Jacqueline. 2005. Sweet Home Alabama: A Linguistic Analysis of Southern
    Dialect in the Media.

Wikipedia.com

LEARNING SOCIAL GREETINGS IN MULTIPLE LANGUAGES

Social greetings have been studied in linguistic anthropology. They vary from culture to culture. According to Fonarow, social greetings are used with a specific format, or formulaic. They are used in many situations, for example, on the phone, in foyers at music gigs, and in the Sahara desert when two nomads (Tuareg or "blue men") meet (Fonarow 2005).

Social greetings can be used to break the ice, or bridge a gap between two people coming together. They can be an inquiry of well being, a religious invocation, a greeting, and identification of parties involved. They can be used to gather information, either about current events, or about a specific topic. They have a specific purpose, norms, and end. The people using the social greetings can be family, friends, business associates, or strangers. (Fonarow 2005).

It can be very useful for the therapist to learn a few social greetings in many languages, so at the very least, s/he can bridge the gap, begin building rapport, and show respect.

Here are a few.

Afrikaans:

Halo.	Hello.
Hoe gaan dit met jou?	How are you.
Elk is bly om jou te ontmoet.	Fine. Thank you.

Amharic (Ethiopia):

Selame, Endemenshe (to female)	Hello, How are you?
Selame, Endemene (to male)	Hello, How are you?
Dehena, Amesgnelhu	I am fine, thank you.

Arabic:

Kayfa Haluk?	How are you?
Anaa bikhayr shukran	Fine. Thank you.

Armenian:

Barev, Inchpes es?	Hi, How are you?
Es lav em, Shnorakalutun	I am fine. Thank you.

Bahasa Indonesia:

Apa kabar?	How are you?
Saya baik-baik saja, terima kasih.	I am fine. Thank you.

Blackfoot:

Tsa nii tap pii wa   How are you? (what is happening)(how are things)
Nii tah tso kin moh ts   Tso ka pii   I am fine. Thank you. (I feel good) (good)

Brazilian Portuguese:

Oi. Tudo bem?   Hi, How are you? (All well?)
Estou bem, muito obrigado.   I am fine. thank you.

Cantonese:

Nay ho mä?   How are you?
Ho. Do chë.   I am fine. thank you.

Castillian:

¿Cómo está Usted?   How are you?
Estoy bien, gracias.   I am fine. Thank you.

Cherokee (Tsalagi).

Do-hi-tsu   Hi, How are you?
O-s-da, wa-do   I am fine. Thank you.

Diné (Navajo):

Haalá nít'é?   How are you?
Yá'ánísht'ééh, Ahéhee'   I am fine. Thank you.

Dutch:

Hallo, Hoe gaat het?   Hello there, how are you?
Goed, dank u.   I am fine. Thank you.

Farsi (Western):

Haal-e shomaa chetor ast?   How are you?
Khoobam. Moteshakeram.   I am fine. Thank you.

French:

Comment allez vous?   How are you?
Je vais bien, merci.   I am fine. Thank you.

German:

Wie geht esIhnen?   How are you?
Mir geht is gut, danke.   I am fine. Thank you.

Greek:

Ti KAnis?   How are you?
EEme kaLA efhariSTO.   I am fine. Thank you.

Haitian Creole:

Kòman ou ye?   How are you?
M pa pi mal, mèsi.   I am fine. Thank you.

Hawaiian:

Pehea 'oe?   How are you?
Maika'i au, mahalo.   I am fine. Thank you.

Hindi:

Ap kaisee hein?   How are you?
Mein Theek hoon, dhanyavAd.   I am fine. Thank you.

Igbo (Nigeria):

Kedu ka idi?   How are you?
Adi m nma. Ndewo.   I am fine. Thank you.

Italian:

Come sta?   How are you?
Sto bene grazie.   I am fine. Thank you.

Japanese:

O-genki desu ka?   How are you?
Genki desu.   I am fine. Thank you.

Kiswahili:

Habari yako. Habari yako.   How are you?
Habari mzuri, asante.   I am fine. Thank you.

Korean:

Ahn nyong ha se yo?	How are you?
Neh jal I soumni da,	I am fine.
Gahm sa hahm ni da	Thank you.

Mandarin:

Nín hao ma?	How Are You?
Wo hen hao, xiè xiè nín.	I am fine. Thank you.

Oriya (India):

Kemiti acha	How are you?
Mu Bhala Achi, Dhanyabad.	I am fine. Thank you.

Polish:

Jak siê Pani powodzi?	How are you doing?
Dziêkujê, całkiem niezle.	I am fine. Thank you.

Portuguese (Brazil):

Oi. Tudo bem?	Hi, How are you? (All well)
Estou bem, muito obrigado.	I am fine. Thank you.

Portuguese (Portugal):

Como Você Está?	How are you?
Anos. Eu estou bem. Obrigado.	I am fine. Thank you.

Russian:

Zdractvuy, Kak ti?	Hi, How are you?
Horosho, Spasibo.	I am fine. Thank you.

Spanish (Latin):

¿Cómo está Usted?	How are you?
Estoy bien, gracias.	I am fine. Thank you.

Tagolog:

Kumasta ka na?	How are you?
Mabuti naman, salamat po.	I am fine. Thank you.

Thai:

Khun sa-bye' dee rue. How are you?
Chan sa-bye' dee. Khorb' khun. I am fine. Thank you.

Tsalagi (Cherokee):

Do-hi-tsu How are you?
O-s-da, wa-do I am fine. Thank you.

Turkish:

Salam Aleikon, Hales yackchidi (fill this in)
Alaha shoker yackchidi, Sagolasan Thank God, I'm fine. Be healthy (thank you).
Nasilsiniz? How are you?
Lyiyim tesekkur ederim. I am fine. Thank you.

Vietnamese:

Bà có khòe không? How are you, mam?
Da tòi khòe, cám on Ông. I am fine, thank you, sir.

Welsh:

Sut ych chi? How are you?
Yn iawn, diolch. I am fine. Thank you.

Wolof (Senegal):

Jàmm ngaam? Na nga def? Hello. (You have peace?) How are you?
Jàmm rek. I am fine. Thank you. (only peace).

Yoroba (Nigeria)

Bawoni How are things going?
Dada ni It is good.

References:

Fonarow, Wendy, PhD, Linguistic Anthropologist, Glendale Community College, CA
    Lectures and notes on Culture and Communication 2005.

Thrash, Jacqueline.
    Social greetings extracted from translations of each language, in Common Phrase
    Translations series.

CONCLUSION

In conclusion, we have reviewed the history of the Civil Rights Act of 1964, and seen the phenomenal contributions of African Americans to American culture, legislation and technology. As a result of this legislation, we have seen benefits for Americans with Disabilities, whether American-born or immigrated. We have also seen the benefit of Executive Order 13166, designed for "Improving Access to Services for Persons with Limited English Proficiency".

We have reviewed the meaning, need and importance of cultural competency as well as the methods for improving one's own understanding and appreciation of other cultures.

We have seen that language is an integral part of culture whether oral, gestured or written. In addition, we have discussed the nexuses of cultural, medical anthropology, linguistics and allied health, and have seen that native language acquisition is an appropriate method to both increase the therapist's cultural competency and to improve the therapeutic outcome with the client. Also, we have reviewed the current literature regarding language translations and caring for patients and clients of other cultures.

For the therapy student, we have demonstrated the importance and necessity of learning social greetings, as well as evaluation and treatment phrases in one's field in multiple languages. For the treating therapist, who has seen the challenges of language barriers in the workplace, we have provided a viable resource for providing high-quality and effective therapy treatment to clients with limited English proficiency in their native language.

I sincerely hope that you find this book extremely helpful in your everyday therapy treatment. I understand the weight of the contribution that therapists provide to their clients' lives, and I understand that the clients may only have this one opportunity to improve. Therefore, is my hope and desire that we can limit the negative effects of the language barrier, and give our non-English-speaking clients the opportunity to be the best that they can be by providing treatment in *their* native languages.

Again I must thank the numerous translators for their generosity and dedication to this project. I would not have been able to translate the occupational, physical, and speech therapy phrases to so many languages all by myself. Again, I must thank the many people who have shared their culture and language with me, and encouraged me in my cultural and scholastic education.

TRANSLATIONS:

These are examples of languages in the full forty language versions:
>Common Phrase Translation: Occupational Therapy,
>Common Phrase Translation: Physical Therapy, and
>Common Phrase Translation: Speech Therapy.

From English to:

African American Vernacular English (AAVE)
Afrikaans
Amharic (Ethiopia)
Arabic
Armenian
Bahasa Indonesia
Blackfoot
Brazilian Portuguese
Bulgarian
Cantonese
Castillian
Diné (Navajo)
Dutch
Farsi (Western)
French
German
Greek
Hindi
Igbo (Nigeria)
Italian
Japanese
Kiswahili

Korean
Mandarin
Mandingo
Maori (New Zealand)
Oriya (India)
Polish
Portuguese
Punjabi
Russian
Spanish (Latin)
Tagalog
Thai
Tsalagi (Chereokee)
Turkish
Vietnamese
Wageman (Australia)
Welsh
Wolof (Senegal)
Yoruba

APPENDICES
A and B

Appendix A: Countries and Languages

Continent Or Area	Country	Living Languages Spoken	Present in this Book
AFRICA			
	Algeria	18	Arabic, French
	Angola	41	Portuguese
	Benin	54	French
	Botswana	28	Africaans, English
	British Indian Ocean Territory	1	English
	Burkina Faso	68	French
	Burundi	3	French, Swahili
	Cameroon	279	Arabic, English, French
	Cape Verde Islands	2	Portuguese
	Central African Republic	69	French
	Chad	132	Arabic, French
	Comoros	7	Arabic, French
	Congo	62	French
	Côte d'Ivoire	78	French
	Democratic Republic of the Congo	214	French
	Djibouti	5	Arabic, French
	Egypt	11	Arabic
	Equatorial Guinea	14	French, Spanish
	Eritrea	12	Arabic, English, Italian
	Ethiopia	84	Amharic, English
	Gabon	41	French
	Gambia	9	English, Wolof
	Ghana	79	English
	Guinea	34	French
	Guinea-Bissau	21	Portuguese
	Kenya	61	English, Swahili
	Lesotho	5	English
	Liberia	30	English
	Libya	9	Arabic
	Madagascar	13	French
	Malawi	14	Afrikaans, English
	Mali	50	French, Wolof
	Mauritania	6	Wolof
	Mauritius	6	English, French
	Mayotte	4	French, Swahili

Continent Or Area	Country	Living Languages Spoken	Present in this Book
	Morocco	11	Arabic, Spanish
	Mozambique	43	Portuguese, Swahili
	Namibia	28	Afrikaans, English
	Niger	21	Arabic, French
	Nigeria	510	English, Ibo (Igbo)
	Réunion	3	French
	Rwanda	3	English, French
	Saint Helena	1	English
	São Tomé e Príncipe	4	Portuguese
	Senegal	36	French, Wolof
	Seychelles	3	English, French
	Sierra Leone	24	English
	Somalia	13	Arabic, English, Swahili
	South Africa	24	Afrik., Eng., Hindi, Swahili
	Sudan	134	Arabic
	Swaziland	4	English
	Tanzania	128	Arabic, English, Swahili
	Togo	39	French
	Tunisia	8	Arabic, French
	Uganda	43	English, Hindi, Swahili
	Zambia	41	Afrikkans, English,
	Zimbabwe	19	English

THE AMERICAS

Continent Or Area	Country	Living Languages Spoken	Present in this Book
	Anguilla	2	English
	Antigua and Barbuda	2	English
	Argentina	27	Spanish, Welsh
	Aruba	3	Dutch, English
	Bahamas	2	English
	Barbados	2	English
	Belize	8	English, Spanish
	Bermuda	1	English
	Bolivia	36	Spanish
	Brazil	188	Brazilian Portuguese
	British Virgin Islands	2	English
	Canada	85	Blackfoot, Eng., Fren., Germ.
	Cayman Islands	1	English
	Chile	11	Spanish
	Colombia	80	Spanish
	Costa Rica	9	Spanish

Continent Or Area	Country	Living Languages Spoken	Present in this Book
	Cuba	2	Spanish
	Dominica	3	English
	Dominican Republic	4	Haitian Creole, Eng. Span.
	Ecuador	23	Spanish
	El Salvador	5	Spanish
	Falkland Islands	1	English
	French Guiana	10	French
	Greenland	2	-----
	Grenada	3	English
	Guadeloupe	4	Eng. French, Haitian Creole
	Guatemala	54	Spanish
	Guyana	16	English
	Haiti	2	French, Haitian Creole
	Honduras	10	English, Spanish
	Jamaica	3	English
	Martinique	2	French
	Mexico	291	Spanish
	Montserrat	2	English
	Netherlands Antilles	4	Dutch, English
	Nicaragua	7	Spanish
	Panama	14	Spanish
	Paraguay	20	German, Spanish
	Peru	93	Spanish
	Puerto Rico	3	English, Spanish
	Saint Kitts and Nevis	2	English
	Saint Lucia	2	English
	Saint Pierre and Miquelon	2	English, French
	Saint Vincent and the Grenadines	2	English
	Suriname	16	Dutch
	Trinidad and Tobago	6	English, Spanish
	Turks and Caicos Islands	2	English
	U.S. Virgin Islands	1	English
	Uruguay	2	Spanish
	USA	162	Blackfoot, Cherokee, English Hawaiian, Navajo, Russian Spanish,

The United States has many people who have made this their home. Please refer to language of country of origin.

| | Venezuela | 40 | Spanish |

Continent Or Area	Country	Living Languages Spoken	Present in this Book
ASIA			
	Afghanistan	47	Farsi
	Armenia	6	Armenian
	Azerbaijan	14	Armenian
	Bahrain	3	Arabic
	Bangladesh	39	Hindi
	Bhutan	24	-----
	Brunei	17	Mandarin, English
	Cambodia	21	English, French
	China	235	Mandarin
	Cyprus	4	Armenian, Greek, Turkish
	East Timor	19	Portuguese
	Georgia	12	-----
	India	415	English, Hindi, Oriya, Punjabi
	Indonesia	737	(see below)
	Java and Bali	20	Mandarin
	Kalimantan	83	-----
	Sumatra	49	-----
	Maluku	129	-----
	Nusa Tenggara	73	-----
	Papua	269	-----
	Sulawesi	114	-----
	Iran	75	Armenian, Farsi (W)
	Iraq	21	Arabic, Armenian, Farsi (W)
	Israel	33	Amharic, Arabic, Armenian English, Russian
	Japan	15	Japanese, Korean
	Jordan	9	Arabic, Armenian
	Kazakhstan	7	German
	Korea, North	1	Korean
	Korea, South	2	Korean
	Kuwait	3	Arabic
	Kyrgyzstan	3	Russian
	Laos	82	-----
	Lebanon	6	Arabic, Armenian Armenian, French

Continued next page....

Continent Or Area	Country	Living Languages Spoken	Present in this Book
	Malaysia	140	(see below)
	Sarawak	46	-----
	Peninsular	40	Mandarin, English
	Sabah	54	-----
	Maldives	1	-----
	Mongolia	13	Mandarin, Russian
	Myanmar	108	-----
	Nepal	123	Hindi
	Oman	13	Arabic, Farsi (W)
	Pakistan	72	English
	Palestinian West Bank and Gaza	4	Arabic
	Philippines	171	Tagalog, English, Spanish, Mandarin,
	Qatar	3	Arabic, Farsi (W)
	Russia	101	(see below)
	(Asia)	42	Korean, Mandarin
	(Europe)	59	Russian, Greek, German
	Saudi Arabia	5	Arabic
	Singapore	21	Mandarin, English
	Sri Lanka	7	English
	Syria	15	Arabic, Armenian
	Taiwan	22	Mandarin, Japanese
	Tajikistan	9	Farsi (W)
	Thailand	74	Thai, Japanese Vietnamese, Mandarin, Korean
	Turkey	34	(see below)
	(Asia)	23	Turkish
	(Europe)	11	Armenian, Bulgarian, Greek
	Turkmenistan	3	-----
	United Arab Emirates	7	Arabic, Farsi (W)
	Uzbekistan	7	Turkish
	Viet Nam	102	Vietnamese
	Yemen	8	Arabic
EUROPE			
	Albania	7	Greek
	Andorra	3	French, Spanish
	Austria	9	German
	Belarus	1	-----
	Belgium	9	Dutch, French, German (some Portuguese, Spanish)

Continent Or Area	Country	Living Languages Spoken	Present in this Book
	Bosnia and Herzegovina	4	----- (some Italian, German, and Turkish)
	Bulgaria	11	Bulgarian, Turkish
	Croatia	6	Italian
	Czech Republic	8	German, Russian
	Denmark	8	German
	Estonia	2	-----
	Finland	12	-----
	France	29	Dutch, French, Greek, Italian, Portuguese, Spanish (Castilian)
	Germany	27	German
	Gibraltar	2	English, Spanish (Castilian)
	Greece	14	Bulgarian, Greek, Turkish
	Hungary	12	German
	Iceland	3	-----
	Ireland	5	English
	Italy	33	French, German, Greek, Italian,
	Latvia	5	-----
	Liechtenstein	3	German
	Lithuania	4	-----
	Luxembourg	3	French, German
	Macedonia	9	Turkish
	Malta	3	English
	Moldova	5	Bulgarian
	Monaco	3	French
	Netherlands	15	Dutch
	Norway	11	-----
	Poland	11	German
	Portugal	7	Portuguese
	Romania	15	Bulgarian, German, Greek, Turkish
	Russia (see ASIA)		
	San Marino	2	Italian
	Serbia and Montenegro	11	Bulgarian
	Slovakia	10	German
	Slovenia	4	Italian
	Spain	13	Spanish (Castilian)

Continent Or Area	Country	Living Languages Spoken	Present in this Book
	Sweden	15	-----
	Switzerland	12	French, German, Italian
	Turkey (see ASIA)		
	Ukraine	10	Greek
	United Kingdom	12	English, French, Welsh
	Vatican State	2	Italian
THE PACIFIC			
	American Samoa	2	English
	Australia	231	English, Wageman
	Cook Islands	5	English
	Fiji	10	English
	French Polynesia	9	French
	Guam	2	English
	Kiribati	2	English
	Marshall Islands	2	English
	Micronesia	18	English
	Nauru	3	English
	New Caledonia	39	French
	New Zealand	4	English, Maori
	Niue	2	English
	Norfolk Island	2	English
	Northern Mariana Islands	4	English
	Palau	4	English
	Papua New Guinea	820	English
	Pitcairn	2	English
	Samoa	2	English
	Solomon Islands	70	English
	Tokelau	2	English
	Tonga	3	English
	Tuvalu	2	-----
	Vanuatu	109	English, French
	Wallis and Futuna	3	English

Appendix B: Cultural Competency Resources

Administration on Aging:

http://www.aoa.dhhs.gov

> Administration on Aging; Dept of Health and Human Services.

Anthropology:

http://www.Plagiocephaly.org

http://www.glendale.edu/anthropology/fonarow.htm

http://www.pasadena.edu/

http://anthro.fullerton.edu/

http://www2.sjsu.edu/depts/anthropology/swaa/

http://www.aaanet.org/

Cultural Awareness:

http://www.norinedresser.com/

> Professional consultant and speaker who presents cultural awareness training in
> In business and educational and service settings. Author of <u>Multicultural Manners</u>
> and <u>Multicultural Celebrations</u>. Folklorist, and University Professor, Speaker and
> Workshop Educator.

http://www.calstatela.edu/faculty/ggalant/

> Geri-Ann Galanti, PhD Anthropology Associate Professor, CSU Los Angeles,
> Department of Anthropology and CSU Dominguez Hills, Department of Nursing
> and author of <u>Caring for Patients from Different Cultures</u>. Speaker, and
> Workshop Educator.

http://www.nova.edu/~stevec/PHT7140.html

> Course in Cultural Diversity in Health Care, by Steve Cohen
> Syllabus listed on website. stevec@nova.edu

http://www.diversityrx.org/HTML/DIVRX.htm

http://www.xculture.org/training/overview/cultural

http://www.xculture.org/resource/reading/index.html

Cross Cultural Health Care Program

Health and Human Services:

http://www.air.org/cecp/cultural

US Dept of Health and Human Services Health Resources and Service Administration: HRSA Bureau of Health Professionals

Language:

César J. Vallejo, Spanish Assistant Professor, Pasadena City College Languages Division, 1570 E. Colorado Blvd, Pasadena CA 91106 cjvallejo@pasadena.edu

Medical Care:

http://www.amsa.org/programs/gpit/cultural.cfm

American Medical Student Association

The Center for Cross Cultural Health
410 Church street, Suite W227, Minneapolis, MN 55455
http://www.umn.edu/ccch/

Cross Cultural Health Care Program
270 South Hanford Street, Suite 100, Seattle, WA 98134
Phone: (206) 860-0329
http://www.xculture.org/

Department of Health and Human Services
Health Resources and Services Administration
Bureau of Primary Health Care
4350 East-West Highway, Bethesda, MD 20814

Office of Minority Health
PO Box 37337, Washington DC 20013-7337
Phone: (800) 444-6472
www.info@omhrc.gov

County of Los Angeles
Commission of Human Relations
320 West Temple Street, Los Angeles, C 90012
Phone: (213) 974-7611
Interface International

Provides publications and training tools
Suzanne Salimbene, Ph.D.
3821 East State Street, Suite 197, Rockford, IL 61108
Phone: (815) 965-7535
e-mail: IF4YOU@aol.com

National Casa Project
100 W Harrison St, North Tower, Ste 500, Seattle, WA 98119
Phone: (800) 628-3233
http://www.casanet.org/

BaFa-BaFa Simulation Training System
218 Twelfth Street, Del Mar, CA 92014-0901
Resources for Cross-cultural Health Care
http://www.diversityrx.org/

University of Washington Ethnic Medicine Guide
http://www.hslib.washington.edu/clinical/ethnomed/

National Urban League
Phone: (212) 310-9000
http://www.nul.org/

African Community Health and Social League
Phone: (510) 839-7764
http://www.progway.org/ACHSS.html

Association of Asian Pacific Community Health Organizations
Phone: (510) 272-9536
http://www.aapcho.org

National Coalition of Hispanic Health and Human Services Organizations
Phone: (202) 387-5000
http://www.cossmho.org

Center for American Indian and Alaskan Native Health
Phone: (410) 955-6931
http://ih1.sph.jhu.edu/cnah/

Continued next page...

http://www.sunyit.edu/library/html/culturedmed/bib/cultcomp/

Culture Med: "CulturedMed" at the Peter J.Cayan Library at SUNYIT is a web
    site and a resource center of print materials promoting culturally-competent health
    care for refugees and immigrants.
    Jacquelyn Coughlan, Librarian, SUNYIT Cayan Library jackie@sunyit.edu

Nursing:

http://www.nursingworld.org/

    American Nurses Association
    Leonard, B. (May 31, 2001) "Quality Nursing Care Celebrates Diversity" Online
    Journal of Issues in Nursing

Occupational Therapy:

Jacqueline Thrash, thrash@pinkiemae.com

http://www2.sjsu.edu/ot/edcara@casa.sjsu.edu

    San Jose State University, San Jose CA: OT Program

http://www.ups.edu/x3024.xml

    University of Puget Sound, Tacoma Washington: OT Program

http://www-home.cr.duq.edu/~munoz/
http://www.home.duq.edu/~munoz/research.html

    Jaime Phillip Muñoz, MS OTR, FAOTA Instructor, Occupational Therapy
    Department at Duquesne University in Pittsburg PA
    Co-founder of TODOS, The National Network of Hispanic Practitioners
    munoz@duq.edu

http://www.aota.org/general/sitesearch.asp?qu=cultural+competency&submit1=Go

    American Occupational Therapy Association
    Links to articles and member area regarding Cultural Competency

Physical Therapy:

http://www.ups.edu/x3020.xml

    University of Puget Sound, Tacoma Washington: PT Program

http://www.apta.org/AM/Template.cfm?Section=Search&template=/CM/HTMLDisplay.
cfm&ContentID=22724

American Physical Therapy Association
Tips on how to increase Cultural Competency

Bender, Denise Gaffigan; <u>Physical Therapy education in the new millennium:
Patient diversity plays a pivotal role in shaping our professional future</u>. Journal of
Physical Therapy Education Winter 2002.

Speech Language Pathology:

http://www.asha.org/default.htm

American Speech-Language-Hearing Association
Disabilities in Culturally and Linguistically Diverse Populations
Disabilities in Culturally and Linguistically Diverse Populations Communication
Development and Disorders in Multicultural Populations: Reading and Related
Materials Cho, S-J., Singer, H.S., & Brenner, M. (2000). ...

http://www.asha.org/about/leadership-projects/multicultural/readings/disabilities.htm -
7.0KB –
ASHA Web Site

Focused Initiative: Culturally and Linguistically Diverse Populations
Focused Initiative: Culturally & Linguistically Diverse Populations Using
information obtained from ASHA members, the Legislative Council and
Executive Board collaborated to identify issues of concern related to ...
*http://www.asha.org/about/leadership-projects/multicultural/recruit/ ficld.htm -
5.5KB - ASHA Web Site*

Ted Levatter, SLP CCC, Professor, Glendale Community College, Glendale CA
tedl@glendale.edu

About the Authors

Jacqueline (Bell) Thrash, OTR.

Thrash's introduction to working with the disabled was in an independent living setting, through referrals from The Center for Independent Living, in Berkeley CA. In the early 1980s, she provided personal care for young adults who were living in the community. Upon the recommendation of one of her spinal cord injured clients, SJ, she later pursued and received her BS OT at San Jose State University in 1986. She has worked in Arizona, Northern California (SF Bay Area); Central California (Visalia, Tulare, Porterville), and Southern California (Ridgecrest, Los Angeles, and San Fernando Valley). Her clinical concentration has been primarily acute rehabilitation with an emphasis on working with clients with spinal cord injuries, tramautic brain injuries, and other neurological diagnoses. She has also practiced in the home care, skilled nursing, and adult day health care settings. She had her own business, Living Skills Therapy in Oakland CA for nearly ten years. In addition to developing education material in OT school, she spoke at the OTAC conference as a student in 1982, and has continued with education in the clinical setting whenever possible. She was recently inducted into the National Anthropology Honors Society Lambda Alpha at Pasadena City College, and presented a paper on linguistics to the Southwest Anthropology Association in April 2006.

César J. Vallejo, MA Spanish Literature: Golden Age-USC. Assisant Professor at Pasadena City College-Languages Division-Spanish. Professor Vallejo was born in Columbia, South America. He has taught Spanish at USC, Santa Monica College, Flintridge Sacred Heart Academy, and at Los Angeles Trade Technical College. He has studied classical languages, Latin and Greek, in Colombia, and Philosophy in Palermo, Italy, and modern languages: Spanish, English, and Italian. He has also made translations for PCC Nursing program brochures and for the Pacific Asia Museum Program Schedules.

Guy McCormack, OTR PhD FAOTA. Dr. McCormack is the department chair of the OT program at University of Missouri-Columbia. He has previously headed the OT department at Samuel Merritt College in Oakland CA, and instructed for many years at San Jose State Univesity. McCormack is best known by students and clinicians for his work in Mind Body Interventions, Therapeutic Touch, and Use of Eastern Medicine Techniques (Meridians, Acupressure, etc) during clinical treatment. McCormack received his PhD from Saybrook Graduate School and Research Center in San Francisco CA in 1999; his MS from Ohio State University-Columbus OH in 1975, and his BS OT from University of Puget Sound in Tacoma Washington in 1972.

Roger Williams, RPT, MPH. As one of the founding faculty members of the University of Puget Sound (UPS) Physical Therapy Program, Mr. Williams is responsible for the clinical education program in the physical therapy curriculum. He entered the physical therapy field in 1972 and his experience as a physical therapist covers all areas of patient care with particular depth in adult rehabilitation. He is active in research into clinical functional outcome measures and documentation. He is also a University mediator. He is credentialed as a clinical instructor by the American Physical Therapy Association and has published work in the Journal of Physical Therapy Education. He received his BS Physical Therapy, from St. Louis University, in1972, and his MPH fromUniversity of Minnesota in 1975. He joined the UPS faculty in 1976. He can be reached by email at: rwilliams@ups.edu

Ted Levatter, SLP, MA, CCC. Professor Levatter has been a California licensed board certified speech pathologist since 1984. He has had experience working in the nursing home setting for various agencies and has been a full time Professor of Speech at Glendale Community College for the twenty years where he teaches courses in Public Speaking, Voice and Diction, and Oral Interpretation of Literature. He also maintains his own private practice in North Hollywood where he specializes in working with children and adults who stutter. He received his Master's Degree in Speech Pathology from California State University-Los Angeles in 1983.

Photographics by Jennifer Thrash, of Pinkie Mae & Co.
http://www.pinkiemae.com